# RME
## for Scotland

Joe Walker

DYNAMIC
LEARNING

HODDER
GIBSON
AN HACHETTE UK COMPANY

**Acknowledgements**
The author would like to thank Lorna and David, again, who once more accepted my self-imposed seclusion while completing this material and just seem to have endless patience with me… and not just in terms of book-writing.

Thanks are also due to Cammy Mackenzie for allowing me to use his story in the book, and to John and Lorna Norgrove for allowing me to use Linda's story and for commenting upon its first draft.

Thanks to all at Hodder Gibson, particularly to John Mitchell.

Again, thanks to the pupils of Liberton High School who have this material tried out on them as it is being written, and who often make very helpful suggestions which result in useful changes.

The Publishers would like to thank the following for permission to reproduce copyright material:

**Photo credits**
p.1 © Zalmai/ Getty Images; p.2 ©Vibe Images/Fotolia; p.3 ©Jules Frazier /Photodisc/Getty Images; p.4 © Cameron Mackenzie; p.5 ©Rue des Archives/ Tall/Mary Evans; p.6 © Sunitha Pilli / iStockphoto; p.7 © Elizabeth Hayes; p.8 © Local History Centre, Leisure and Culture Dundee; p.9 ©Graeme Robertson/Getty Images; p.10 ©Pastor Sam /Flickr/Getty Images; p.11© Science Facton/Getty Images; p.12 © Imagestate Media (John Foxx); p.13 © Marc Cecchetti /Fotolia; p.14 © Norgrove Family via British Foreign Office / AP Photo; p.16 © Zalmai / Getty Images; p.17 ©Tomy – Fotolia; p.18 © Paul Chesley/Getty Images; p.19 ©Tomy – Fotolia; p.20 © Christine Osborne/Corbis; p.21 © Kablonk Micro- Fotolia; p.22 (left) © Piotr Sikora- Fotolia, (right) © George Doyle/Stockbyte/Getty Images; p.23 © Danny Lawson/Press Association Images/ NUS Scotland; p.24 © Jeff Greenberg/Alamy; p.27 ©Rebecca van Ommen/ Getty; p.28 © TheFinalMiracle - Fotolia.com; p.30 © Apex News and Pictures Agency/Alamy; p.31 © Jane Wynne Wilson/British Humanist Association/www.humanism.org.uk; p.32 © Scott S. Warren/National Geographic Society/Corbis; p.33 © Imagestate Media (John Foxx); p.34 © Harry Price/Mary Evans p.35 © Sandra Cunningham – Fotolia; p.36 © Frank Saragnese/Getty; p.37 © Ryan McVay/Photodisc/Getty Images; p.38 (top) © Jonathan Hordle/Rex Features, (bottom) ©Vladislav Ociacia/Fotolia; p.40 ©Mary Evans; p.41 © John Worth/British Humanist Association; p.42 © Christine Mariner/Design Pics/Corbis; p.43 © Imagestate Media (John Foxx); p.45 © Dave Walker; p.46 ©Pasieka/Science Photo Library; p.47 © Ella Austin; p.48 © Nick Koudis/Photodisc/Getty Images / Professional Science 72; p.49 © Roman Milert - Fotolia p.50 © Imagestate Media (John Foxx); p.51 © 3355m / Fotolia.com; p.52 © BAGUS INDAHONO/epa/Corbis; p.53 ©StockTrek/Photodisc/Getty Images; p.54 © Anton Prado PHOTO - Fotolia. com; p.55 © Yosef – Fotolia; p.56 © Numb/Alamy; p.57 © Rixie – Fotolia; p.59 ©Laguna Design/Science Photo Library; p.60 © wrangler – Fotolia; p.61 © stocker1970 – Fotolia; p.62 © Stephen Finn/Fotolia; p.63 © Roman Milert – Fotolia; p.64 © Elizabeth Hayes; p.65 © ayazad – Fotolia; p.66 © Muhannad Fala'ah/Stringer/Getty Images; p.67 © ayazad – Fotolia; p.68 © shaiith – Fotolia; p.69 © Bartek Wrzesniowski /Alamy; p.70 © World History Archive / TopFoto; p.71 © Image Source/ Getty Images; p.73 (top) © Tjui Tjioe – Fotolia, (bottom) © FAROOQ KHAN/epa/Corbis; p.74 © Ocean/Corbis; p.75 Blend Images RM/ Getty Images; p.76 © Images & Stories / Alamy; p.77 © Imagestate Media Partners Limited - Impact Photos / Alamy; p.78 © Orhan Çam – Fotolia; p.79 © Corbis; p.80 © Topsy 1 / Alamy; p.81 © Bernard Bisson/Sygma/ Corbis; p.82 © Roger Harris/Science Photo Library; p.83 © Bernard Bisson/Sygma/Corbis; p.84 © Russell Kord / Alamy; p.85 © Pereri/Fotolia; p.86 © Mary Evans; p.87 © Russi & Morelli – Fotolia; p.88–9 ©Carolina Biological Supply, Co/Visuals Unlimited, Inc./Science Photo Library; p.90 ©David McNew/Getty Images; p.91 © Mauro Fermariello/Science Photo Library; p.92 © Jason Horowitz/Corbis; p.93 © Laguna Design/Science Photo Library/ Corbis; p.94 © Life in View/Science Photo Library; p.95 ©Gaetan Bally/Press Association; p.96 © David Chesin/Press Association; p.97 ©2009 SeanBreslinPhotography/Getty Images; p.98 © THE SCOTSMAN/ CORBIS SYGMA; p.99 © David Robertson / Alamy; p.100 © John McKenna / Alamy; p.101 © Andrew Holt / Alamy; p.102 © Marka/SuperStock; p.103 © Adam Woolfitt/Corbis; p.104 © Corbis; p.105 © www.BibleLandPictures.com / Alamy; p.106 © Shai Ginott/CORBIS; p.107 © Ahmad Yusni/epa/ Corbis; p.108 ©Chung Sung-Jun/Getty Images; p.109 ©2009 SeanBreslinPhotography/ Getty Images; p.110 © Sanjeev Syal / Demotix/Demotix/ Corbis; p.111 © Interfoto/Mary Evans; p.112 © Piotr Pawinski – Fotolia; p.113 © Robert King/ Getty Images; p.114 © WildCountry/CORBIS; p.115 © E&E Image Library/Photo Library/Getty Images; p.116 © Jim Richardson/Getty Images; p.117 © Arif Iqbal / Alamy; p.118 © Mary Evans Picture Library; p.119 © David Cumming/Eye Ubiquitous/Corbis; p.120 © Egmont Strigl/Photo Library/Getty Images; p.121 © Michel Setboun/Corbis; p.122 © Paramount/Rex Features; p.123 © Robert King/Getty Images; p.124 © Joel Stettenheim/CORBIS; p.125 Designed by Berni Georges. Published with permission of The Salvation Army International Headquarters, London UK; p.126 © John Warburton-Lee Photography / Alamy; p.127 © Robert van der Hilst/Corbis; p.128 © NIR ELIAS/Reuters/Corbis.

Although every effort has been made to ensure that website addresses are correct at time of going to press, Hodder Gibson cannot be held responsible for the content of any website mentioned in this book. It is sometimes possible to find a relocated web page by typing in the address of the home page for a website in the URL window of your browser.

Hachette UK's policy is to use papers that are natural, renewable and recyclable products and made from wood grown in sustainable forests. The logging and manufacturing processes are expected to conform to the environmental regulations of the country of origin.

Orders: please contact Bookpoint Ltd, 130 Milton Park, Abingdon, Oxon OX14 4SB. Tel: (44) 01235 827720. Fax: (44) 01235 400454. Lines are open 9.00–5.00, Monday to Saturday, with a 24-hour message answering service. Visit our website at www.hoddereducation.co.uk. Hodder Gibson can be contacted direct on: Tel: 0141 848 1609; Fax: 0141 889 6315; email: hoddergibson@hodder.co.uk

© Joe Walker 2012
First published in 2012 by
Hodder Gibson, an imprint of Hodder Education,
An Hachette UK Company
2a Christie Street
Paisley PA1 1NB

Impression number    5   4   3   2   1
Year                        2014  2013  2012

Cover photo (from left) © CreativeFire/iStockphoto, © Sunitha Pilli/iStockphoto, © Marcus Lindström/iStockphoto
Typeset in FS Albert Light 11.5/14.5 pt by Pantek Media, Maidstone, Kent
Printed in Dubai

A catalogue record for this title is available from the British Library

ISBN: 978 1444 110753

# Contents

Contents mapping grid iv

Introduction vi

**1** **Active belief** 1

**2** **Marking life's stages** 17

**3** **Big questions** 33

**4** **Environmental issues** 49

**5** **Exploring Islam** 65

**6** **Science and religion** 81

**7** **Spring celebrations** 97

**8** **Christianity: A world religion** 113

# Contents mapping grid

| Topic | Beliefs | Values and issues | Practices and traditions | Development of beliefs and values |
|---|:---:|:---:|:---:|:---:|
| **1. Active belief**<br>1 Cameron Mackenzie<br>2 David Livingstone<br>3 Mary Slessor<br>4 John Muir<br>5 Linda Norgrove | ✓ | ✓ | | ✓ |
| **2. Marking life's stages**<br>6 Birth smoking ceremony<br>7 First communion<br>8 Rumspringa<br>9 Marriage<br>10 A Humanist funeral | ✓ | ✓ | ✓ | ✓ |
| **3. Big questions**<br>11 Do ghosts exist?<br>12 Could a robot have rights?<br>13 Does God exist?<br>14 What makes something right or wrong?<br>15 What makes me me? | ✓ | ✓ | | ✓ |
| **4. Environmental issues**<br>16 The rights of nature<br>17 The land<br>18 The oceans<br>19 The atmosphere<br>20 Sustainable living | ✓ | ✓ | | ✓ |

| Topic | Beliefs | Values and issues | Practices and traditions | Development of beliefs and values |
|---|:---:|:---:|:---:|:---:|
| **5. Exploring Islam**<br>**21** Muhammad and Islam<br>**22** Muslim belief<br>**23** Muslim prayer<br>**24** Sunni and Shia<br>**25** Islamic art | ✓ | ✓ | ✓ | ✓ |
| **6. Science and religion**<br>**26** Religious experience<br>**27** Human behaviour<br>**28** Embryo research<br>**29** Genetic engineering<br>**30** Euthanasia | ✓ | ✓ | | ✓ |
| **7. Spring celebrations**<br>**31** Beltane<br>**32** Greek Orthodox Easter<br>**33** Pesach<br>**34** Wesak<br>**35** Vaisakhi | ✓ | | ✓ | |
| **8. Christianity: A world religion**<br>**36** The Iona Community<br>**37** Christians in Russia<br>**38** Christianity in Ethiopia<br>**39** The Salvation Army<br>**40** Christianity in China | ✓ | ✓ | ✓ | ✓ |

# Introduction

This book explores CfE Religious and Moral Education by suggesting topics and ways of approaching the requirements which cover all of the outcomes and experiences (and more) at Level 4.

The Curriculum for Excellence development programme had as one of its central tenets the idea of flexibility for schools and communities as well as individual teachers. Teachers and schools should respond to their own contexts and students in ways which result in quality learning and teaching experiences which are enjoyed by all. The key to good learning and teaching is **quality**. Quite literally, 'it ain't what you do; it's the way that you do it'.

CfE RME effectively has three modes of operating:

- starting with the student and his or her own exploration and analysis of their own beliefs, values and practices
- moving out to the wider community locally and nationally and comparing and contrasting these with the student's own developing beliefs and values
- finally widening out into a global context over time and place thus orienting the student in terms of their own place in the world and therefore their own possible contribution to it.

This means extending learning beyond the local and national context – out into the wider world – and stressing the interconnected nature of our world and the role which all of us can play in making it a better one. This book is therefore a proposed way to go about RME, but it is expected that teachers will adapt the contained resources to suit their needs and the needs of their students in their own context. The aim of this book is to spark your creativity, not box it in.

Each section of the book follows this format:

An **active introductory stimulus** section destined to engage students and get them thinking about the topic area they're about to explore. It's meant to be humorous but not flippant – and it would be best experienced by students themselves, not just by their teacher reading it to them. It would be expected that this should start off discussion and thinking and the whole process of critical reflection.

A **talking and listening** section. This should come right after the stimulus and should be used to help students think about their own responses to the issues raised, express them and also to listen to what's being expressed by others in the class.

A brief bit of **informative text**. This is intentionally brief as this book offers a more exploratory and active approach to learning. This text should be seen as a natural extension of the talking and listening section.

An **active learning** section. This is designed to encourage students to take ownership of their own learning, exploring and reflecting on their learning as they go.

A **progress check** section. This follows the broad principles of 'Assessment for Learning' and is designed to assess learning in active and creative ways, focusing on knowledge, understanding, analysis, evaluation and skills such as critical thinking and reflection.

An **on your own** section. This is designed so that students engage in independent learning activities. These are not just 'finding out more' tasks but ideas which allow students to explore the topics in a variety of ways.

RME should be enjoyable, informative and life-changing (just like all education). Importantly it should help make the world a better place. Thank you for your contributions in helping your students to do just that.

Joe Walker

# Active belief

Growing up in the streets of Paisley, Cammy's teenage life was a troubled one. His stepfather regularly beat up Cammy's mother. One day Cammy could take no more and – finding his stepfather lying drunk on the bedroom floor – Cammy grabbed a hammer and set about him. The man lived… but only just.

Cammy found himself wandering the streets and soon fell into a harsh life of alcohol, drugs and violence. He moved from one job to another, never keeping one for very long. He had a job at a local hairdresser's for a time, where one of his tasks was the regular washing of the owner's wig.

But even here, Cammy repaid the kindness which was being shown by this hairdresser (who else would give someone like Cammy a job?) by regularly stealing from him.

He eventually lost this job and found employment in a slaughterhouse killing animals. They gave him a very large knife to do his work. He found other uses for this knife too – strapping it to his leg on a Saturday night so that he'd be more than ready if any violence broke out. One night, for no reason at all, Cammy attacked a man with this very knife. The man lived… but only just.

Cammy ended up with a two-year jail sentence. On his release he found work driving a taxi, but he still clung to many of his old bad habits. He would regularly drive while heavily drunk or high on drugs. One day a woman got into the back of his cab and started chatting with him. She said: 'I'm getting a message from the other side.' Cammy thought that she must be more spaced out than he was… 'Cammy,' she continued. 'There is a great dark cloud over your life… you must change to become the person God wants you to be.'

Today Cameron Mackenzie is a Church of Scotland minister at the Tron Kirk in Moredun, Edinburgh.

# Cameron: The rest of the story

After he decided to become a minister, Cameron successfully studied at Glasgow University. He has spent a lot of time in Brazil working with street kids. These children have been abandoned by their families and left to fend for themselves on the troubled streets of Brazil's big cities. Often they are no more than babies. Many people treat them as little more than vermin – to be swept off the streets and pushed out of sight. Like young Cammy, many turn to drugs and alcohol to help them cope with the harsh realities of their lives. Cammy still works for Brazil's street kids from here in Scotland.

Cameron met his wife in Brazil. They came back to Scotland where he was minister in Haddington for ten years and now in Moredun, Edinburgh. Cameron believes that he is an example of how anyone can turn their life around and make a positive contribution

to society. Cameron argues that anyone can be forgiven by God for anything they have done – but, once forgiven, your life has to change for the better so that you can make the world a better place.

Cameron has also had to put forgiveness into action himself since becoming a minister. He explains: 'My young brother Alex was stabbed to death on 30 June 1995 in Ferguslie Park in Paisley.

He was just 27 at the time and had a daughter, and my mum and I, who were the only Christians in the family, chose in obedience to Christ to forgive the two men who did this to him.'

## Active Learning

1. How much of a link is there between a troubled life and 'acting out' in socially unacceptable ways? Write down how you think the following *might* sometimes lead to anti-social behaviour:
   - childhood neglect
   - violence in the home
   - alcohol and drug abuse
   - a group of peers who act in anti-social ways
   - lack of parental love and guidance.

2. Christians believe that God will forgive you for anything. They also believe that this isn't a licence to carry on doing what's wrong. Put the following list into the order of most to least difficult to forgive. Discuss the reasons for your choices.
   a. Someone murders your teenage son during a fight in a nightclub.
   b. A doctor kills your baby by giving it the wrong medicine.
   c. A drink-driver hits your mum – she is paralysed for the rest of her life.
   d. A parent in Brazil throws her child out into the street.
   e. Someone stabs your sister – she survives, but with serious mental health problems.
   f. Your neighbour is discovered to have been seriously neglecting her children for many years.
   g. An ambulance driver refuses to go to someone having a suspected heart attack because he is on his tea-break. The person dies.

3. Draw up a list of arguments for and against 'someone like Cameron' becoming a minister. What good can he now do? What example might he set to young people who behave like he used to?

4. Some have said that Cameron's life would make a great movie. Design a poster for a film of Cameron's life.

## Talking and listening

- Why do you think Cammy's young life was such a mess?
- Scotland has a problem with alcohol, drugs and knife violence – what makes people behave in this way?
- Cameron believes that he has been forgiven for his mistakes. Should God forgive everything?
- Do you know anyone who has turned their life around (or would benefit from doing so)?

### On your own

1. Find out more about street children in Brazil and prepare a presentation on the issues. You could look at the following websites for help:
   - www.oxfam.org.uk/ coolplanet/kidsweb/world/ brazil/brazoxf1.htm
   - www.taskbrasil.org.uk/
   - http://gbgm-umc. org/missionstudies/ globalhealth-yth/ streetchildren.htm

2. Read these Bible stories and re-tell them in your own words. What can we learn about forgiveness from these stories?
   - The woman caught in adultery: John 8:1–11
   - The prodigal son: Luke 15:11–32

### Progress Check

1. Answer these questions about Cameron's life.
   a. How did Cammy's early life affect his behaviour?
   b. Why did Cammy end up taking a hammer to his stepfather?
   c. Why do you think Cammy turned to drink and drugs?
   d. Why were Cammy's actions towards the hairdresser so wrong?
   e. Do you think Cammy's story would have had a different ending if the man he'd attacked with the knife had died?
   f. What finally made Cammy change? Why do you think this event was such a powerful one?

2. Draw up a list of questions you would like to ask Cameron about his old and new life. Perhaps you could also think of some questions about forgiveness and the value of turning your life around.

3. There are many Biblical stories about the importance of helping others, such as the Good Samaritan: Luke 10:24–26. Read this story and explain in your own words what it teaches us about who we should help and in what circumstances.

David Livingstone was born in Blantyre in 1813. After studying medicine and theology at Glasgow University, he decided to take his medical skills to Africa and help people there, while also introducing them to the Christian faith.

In Livingstone's day, the slave trade was still very much alive. Raiders would descend upon tribal villages and snatch people away, taking them to the new world as slaves. They would be forced to work for the rest of their lives – bought and sold like animals, and treated little better. While in Africa, Livingstone tried to encourage people back in Europe to question the slave trade and to work to end it. However, like many Christian missionaries of his day, he had to walk a careful path in his actions. Occasionally he had to negotiate with slave traders to gain their trust and even make use of their power to help him in his activities. It is easy to see Livingstone through twenty-first-century eyes, but he did treat those he met on his travels through Africa as fellow human beings, worthy of respect and consideration, and as people who mattered to him and to God.

Livingstone believed that his missionary work was the right thing to do. He did not believe in using any kind of force or trickery to convert local people from their own beliefs to Christianity – he simply taught them about his faith and allowed them to make their own decisions. This led to him becoming trusted by local people. In fact, they thought of him as a powerful healer and often called upon his medical skills.

He was also considered a great explorer – travelling to places that no European had ever been before and sending back reports which inspired people back in the UK and helped them to understand more about the world in which they lived. In Livingstone's day, many Europeans had never met an African and considered them to be nothing more than savages. Livingstone's reports about his life in Africa challenged these beliefs – helping people to see that, no matter the colour of your skin, where you live or your culture, we are all part of the same human family.

Livingstone died in Africa in 1873 and his body was transported back to the UK, where he was buried among the great and the good in Westminster Abbey.

# Slavery then and now

Livingstone uncovered terrible practices towards slaves. In his last journals of 1865 he tells the story of a slave-owner who bought a woman at a slave market one day and then walked her for many miles. She got very tired and could not walk any further. The slave-owner was angry with her because he felt that he had wasted his money buying her. So he killed her on the spot, left her body on the path and walked away.

This kind of practice was quite common, and Livingstone often came across people on his travels who had been abandoned by their owners because they were no longer fit to work. Such people

would usually be close to death – having been severely beaten or simply starved to the point where their body had given up.

Livingstone is still used as an example of opposition to the slave trade today. It may be hard to believe, but there are still slaves in the twenty-first century. Sometimes these may be children sold off by their parents into what they are promised will be a better life – and who often end up working in sweat shops or as child prostitutes.

In many countries debt-slavery is common too. This is where someone borrows money to survive, or perhaps feed their family. When they cannot repay the money they are forced to work – and often this continues for years until the debt is paid off… if it ever is.

## Talking and listening

- Was it right of Livingstone to take Christianity to those who already had different beliefs?
- In those days, slavery was perfectly normal. Why do you think people thought this? What made them change their minds eventually?
- Do you think anyone in the world today lives in slavery?
- How do you think the reports Livingstone sent back to the UK helped people understand the world better?
- Some might argue that Livingstone should have left the local people alone to live their lives their own way. What do you think?

## Active Learning

1. Livingstone believed that taking his Christian faith to others was the right thing to do. Draw up a list of advantages and disadvantages of doing this. How might this have benefited those he came into contact with? How might it have had more negative effects?

2. You can find out about Livingstone's life on the Internet. Make a timeline of his life story and plot his travels on a map of Europe and Africa.

3. Christian missionaries still work in the world today and many have come from Africa to work as missionaries here. What kind of work do these people do? Is their work valuable or out of date?

4. Child and adult slavery still exists today. Find out more about the different kinds of slavery which exist and prepare your own presentation on this topic. Here are some websites which might help you:
   - www.anti-slaverysociety.addr.com/childlabor01.htm
   - http://news.bbc.co.uk/1/hi/in_depth/world/slavery/default.stm
   - http://ngm.nationalgeographic.com/ngm/0309/feature1/
   - www.antislavery.org/english/

**Progress Check**

1. Answer these questions about the life of David Livingstone using the material in this book and other information you have found.
   a. What two skills and talents did Livingstone take to Africa?
   b. What places did Livingstone visit in Africa?
   c. Which landmarks was he the first European to 'discover'?
   d. Where is he buried and what is the significance of this?
   e. How might his reports of what he found in Africa change people's views of people in Africa at the time?
   f. Why do you think he opposed slavery?

2. Make up an interview with Livingstone where you ask him questions about his life and work. You should think about how he might answer these questions.

3. In a group, take turns to state one thing about Livingstone's life. You must not repeat anything you have heard from anyone else in the group, and if you have to pass, you're out. Last one in wins.

David Livingstone

**On your own**

1. Design your own poster which explores an issue of slavery in the world today and encourages people to do something about it.

2. There are many statues, paintings and photographs of Livingstone around the world. Search on the Internet and make a display of your findings to illustrate his life and work.

In 1859 an eleven-year-old girl began work in a Dundee factory. The work was long and hard, and she fitted in whatever learning she could in the little spare time she had. She was a hard-working girl, though it was said that she was a 'wild lassie' too. Her dad was an alcoholic, but her mother was a very religious woman who made sure that Mary attended church and treated both religion and education as important.

At the age of 28, inspired by her hero David Livingstone, Mary arrived in Nigeria (then called Calabar) to begin the missionary work which she would carry out for the rest of her life. Here, she learned the language and culture and soon became well-known for her courage, wisdom and bravery in fighting against practices which she thought were inhuman. Mary was particularly interested in defending the rights of women and children in Nigeria; for example, when a chief died it was quite common to sacrifice his wives so that they could be buried alongside him. Mary did all she could to encourage local people to put an end to this practice.

Mary also fought against the treatment of twins. At the time, the birth of twins was regarded as very bad luck. The twins would often be killed, and their mother hounded out of the village and never allowed to return. In fact, Mary actually rescued a set of twins – a boy and a girl – as they were about to be killed and took them to live with her. Shortly afterwards the boy was taken by the tribespeople and killed, but Mary managed to keep the girl who she named Janie, and brought her up as her own daughter.

Mary would often find children left at her doorstep and did her best to look after them. She also tried to bring an end to other common practices such as cannibalism. Mary did all of these things because she believed that every person was of value to God. In Nigeria she is still remembered as the red-headed woman of great courage who became known as 'white Ma'.

### Talking and listening

- How do you think Mary's early life might have influenced her to become a missionary?
- Why do you think local people might have had such a fear of twins?
- Mary tried to encourage locals to give up traditional practices. Is it right to challenge people's traditional ways?
- In what ways are women still treated unfairly in the world today?
- Why do you think the local people would give their babies to Mary?

## The rights of women and children today

In Mary's day women in Britain were fighting for their rights, such as the right to vote. A year before Mary's death, the First World War began – this would bring great changes to the roles of men and women in Britain. Women now have a far more equal place in British society, though many say that we are still far from achieving complete equality between the sexes.

In economically less developed countries, the rights of women remain an important issue. Domestic violence against women is still common in places where women are seen as the 'property' of their husbands, and the education of girls in many countries still falls far behind the education of boys. In some countries, girl babies are killed at birth because they are considered to be a 'burden' to families. It is thought that they won't be able to work in the way that boys do, and this will mean that the family has to provide a dowry to marry a girl off to another family.

Children also still suffer poor treatment in many countries of the world. Child exploitation and child labour are still common in many places. And, though it may be hard to believe, there are still places in the world today where children may be sacrificed or killed because they are thought to be witches or possessed by evil. It seems that many of the things Mary fought against in the late nineteenth and early twentieth centuries are still with us.

### Active Learning

1. Make your own timeline of Mary's life and plot her travels on a world map and on a map of Nigeria.

2. In what ways are girls and women still treated unfairly compared to men in the world today? Discuss the kinds of things which might happen and then search the Internet to find examples of this for display.

3. Do you think girls in Scotland are treated equally with boys? Write about ways in which the genders might be treated differently, or write about any experiences of differences in treatment you know about.

4. Mary believed that many of the traditional practices of the locals were simply wrong. However, some believe that missionaries such as Mary have no right to interfere in local customs and traditions – no matter how wrong they might seem. Think about the arguments on each side and have a debate about it in class.

Mary Slessor

1. Find out about the history of children being treated badly. In what countries has this happened? What beliefs lie behind it? Are any prejudices towards children still shown today? The following websites might help you:
   - www.scotland.gov.uk/ Topics/People/Young-People/Childrens-Rights
   - www.oxfam.org.uk/ education/resources/rights
   - www.christianaid.org.uk/

2. Find out more about how women's rights can still be an issue in the world today. Draw up a list of the top ten issues which affect women in the world today.

### Progress Check

1. Answer these questions about the life of Mary Slessor:
   a. Mary was born in Aberdeen – where did her family move to?
   b. How did Mary show her commitment to education?
   c. In what ways did Mary try to fit in with the local culture in Nigeria?
   d. What practices linked to the wives of chiefs and twins did Mary fight against?
   e. Why did Mary do the things she did?
   f. What would Mary fight against in today's world?

2. Design an information sheet about the life and work of Mary Slessor.

3. In pairs, take turns to say one word linked to the story of Mary Slessor. After one person says the word, the other person has five seconds to say something linked to this word.

John Muir was born in Dunbar, East Lothian, in 1838. In those days, most people saw nature as something wild and dangerous. They tried to tame it by making it into ordered gardens wherever they could, and conquered it by climbing mountains and taking from it whatever they needed. There was little concern for wild animals or wild places – most people liked the order of 'civilised' places such as towns and cities.

John, however, saw things differently. From childhood he had a love of all things wild and natural and this was to develop into a life's work which saw him help to establish some of the largest natural parks in the world in the USA, and to be celebrated as a national hero there. In fact, on 21 April each year, the state of California – one of the most powerful economies in the world – celebrates John Muir Day.

When he was 11, John's family emigrated to the USA to begin a new life. Here, John discovered great places of natural beauty, and even undertook a one-thousand-mile walk from Indiana to Florida by the wildest route he could find. John believed that nature was of great value – both in itself and in the way in which it could benefit your spiritual life. John believed that you could see the divine in every leaf and every rock. Nature could help you to see yourself and the world the way it really was. He thought that in nature you could truly understand what life was about, which just wasn't possible in places where humans had turned nature into 'civilisation'. John believed that getting back to nature would help anyone to live a much more meaningful life, and so it was important to preserve wild places as much as possible.

Apart from campaigning to set up the great natural parks such as Yosemite, John was also a founder of the Sierra Club – perhaps the world's first ever green organisation. Here in Scotland, the John Muir Trust keeps John's beliefs about nature alive through protecting wild places in our own country. They also help people to learn about, understand and benefit from all things natural. John himself said: 'The clearest way into the universe is through a forest wilderness'.

## 💬 *Talking and listening*

- Do you think of nature as something to be conquered or something to be looked after?
- What might people learn about themselves from experiencing the natural world?
- What evidence is there that nature is mistreated by humans?
- Do you think there is anything 'spiritual' about nature?
- When did you last enjoy being in a natural place?

# Is nature under threat today?

While there are many natural places left in the world, and there are many protected places too, there are also areas of nature which are under threat. The rainforests of the Amazon and south-east Asia are being destroyed at alarming rates. This harms the animals and the people who live there, but may also harm the whole planet by bringing about climate changes on a global scale.

But perhaps we don't need to look so far away to see how human activity is often bad for nature... Land, air and rivers close to our homes may be polluted with chemical substances left over from our modern lifestyles. In fact, our homes themselves may harm nature – building increases to house an ever-growing population and so pushes wild places further and further back. The land we use to grow the food we eat becomes exhausted, and we plunder nature more and more to meet our needs for energy, food and natural resources. Even the jotters you write on in school may be the result of the destruction of a forest somewhere – removing yet another clear way into the universe for us all.

There are many examples of how humans may be harming nature through our very existence. Of course there are organisations trying to put this right, but perhaps – if we are all to benefit from nature in the ways John Muir said we could – we all have to play our part in preserving and protecting it.

## Active Learning

1. Two places owe their existence today to the life of John Muir and his campaigning environmentalism: Yosemite National Park in California and the Munro Schiehallion in Perth and Kinross. Find out more about each of these and prepare a display about them which includes information about their geography, history and how wildlife and humans can benefit from them.

2. Prepare a PowerPoint slideshow of images of nature to show its beauty. Think of suitable music to accompany this slideshow. You could also mix in some images of ways in which humans are harming nature too (and change the background music as necessary).

3. Find out about the continued work of the Sierra Club and the John Muir Trust and write about what you find in your jotters. What do they do today to keep John's beliefs alive? See www.jmt.org/ and www.sierraclub.org/. Perhaps you could also carry out some activity in your school to support one of these organisations.

4. John believed that nature was good for our souls and helped us to understand ourselves more. If possible, take a walk in a natural place and really look around to try to experience what surrounds you. Write about your experience afterwards in prose, poetry or even a song.

1. Answer these questions about John Muir:
   a. In what ways were John's views about nature different to those of most people in his day?
   b. How did John think nature was different to 'human civilisation'?
   c. How did he help to preserve nature in the USA?
   d. Which organisations still keep his memory alive today and how do they do so?
   e. What benefits could nature bring to people, according to John?
   f. In what different ways is John still remembered today?

2. Design a poster encouraging people to think more about how we treat the natural world. You could use a quote from John Muir in your poster.

3. Make up your own crossword about John Muir.

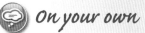 *On your own*

1. Find out about an example of how nature is harmed near where you live. It could be an example of pollution or of building houses or roads in wild places, or simply litter in your school. Write about what you find and suggest ways in which to respond to this.

2. Draw up a list of threats to nature in the world today. You could order these according to how serious/harmful you think they might be.

# Linda Norgrove

Linda Norgrove was brought up on the Isle of Lewis but, in her short life, saw a great many parts of the world. She learned about the cultures and lifestyles of others, helping them to get more out of their situations while living a life 'that mattered'.

Having studied at Aberdeen University and achieving great academic success, she spent time in a university in Mexico as well as doing field work among local people in Uganda. While Linda was an environmental specialist, she was always interested in the people she came into contact with. She devoted her life to helping them, sometimes in situations where life was difficult for them and challenging for her. Her great passion was environmental issues. However, Linda soon realised that there were many times when local people ended up suffering because of projects which tried to help the environment. So her focus changed from the environment to helping the poor.

It was no great surprise, then, when she ended up working for the United Nations in the war-torn and troubled land of Afghanistan in 2005. By early 2010 she was working for an international aid and development agency called DAI.

Her role was to manage and support local people to set up and run projects which help them to support themselves. These projects could be anything from building roads and irrigation projects to finding different jobs for people who had previously been involved in growing poppies (which were turned into opium and found their way onto the world's drugs market). At all times, Linda greatly respected local cultures and traditions – learning the local ways and language and being sensitive to local circumstances. Her respect for the people in Afghanistan earned their respect in turn, both for herself and for the work she was so committed to.

However, on 26 September 2010, Linda was kidnapped. Then on 8 October 2010, during an attempt to rescue her from her kidnappers, Linda's life of service and commitment to others was brought to an end. Her parents have now set up a foundation in her name to continue the work she did on behalf of others in Afghanistan. They hope that by doing this they can keep alive the support for others which was so important to Linda. In 2011, Linda was announced as the winner of the Robert Burns Humanitarian Award in recognition of her work in making the world a better place.

# Helping others

Linda believed that people should be helped to make the most of their lives – no matter what their situation. The conflict in Afghanistan is a complicated one and local people often suffer greatly because of the fighting around them and the political and social implications of the international community's activities there. There is widespread poverty in Afghanistan and this can often affect the lives of women and children most seriously.

In fact, the country has been a troubled one for many years. There have been conflicts with Russia, internal conflict between local people and the Taliban, and now Afghanistan is the focus of international attention as part of what has become known as 'the war on terror'. Despite the dangers and the complexity of the situation, there are many aid agencies and individuals working in the country – and working with local people – to help make the lives of those who live there better. This might involve building schools so that children (especially girls) get the chance to have an education, providing healthcare and helping people to learn important skills such as agriculture.

The organisations present in the country aim to help the people there to get into a position where they can support themselves and run their own affairs in their own way. These organisations are not political and they do not 'take sides' – they are there to help people according to their needs, just as Linda did.

## Talking and listening

- In what ways do you help others?
- What would you be prepared to risk your life to do?
- In what different ways are people in need in the world today?
- What do you know about the conflicts in Afghanistan?
- In what ways might Linda have been in danger in Afghanistan?

## Active Learning

1. Visit the website of the Linda Norgrove Foundation at www. lindanorgrovefoundation.org/ and make a report on what this website aims to do. Perhaps you could do something to help the work of the organisation.

2. Create your own factfile on Afghanistan which contains information about the country's geography and history – including the history of the conflicts which have led to its present-day situation.

3. It is easy to forget that in war-torn places such as Afghanistan life must go on as close to normal as possible for the people who live there. Create a slideshow of positive images showing how the people of Afghanistan are being helped and helping themselves to make life better.

4. Another well-known humanitarian working in Afghanistan is Greg Mortensen. Visit the website of his organisation and write some notes on what he does and why. See www.ikat.org/

## Progress Check

1. Answer these questions about Linda Norgrove:
   a. Where was Linda brought up?
   b. Why did she switch her focus from environmental issues to helping the poor?
   c. What job did she do in Afghanistan?
   d. What kinds of things did this work involve?
   e. How did she show that she was 'sensitive to the local culture'?
   f. What award did she win and why?

2. Create your own poster about the Linda Norgrove Foundation.

3. Make up your own quiz on the life of Linda Norgrove.

## On your own

1. Think about the area you live in. In what ways might people around you be in need? How could you help? Perhaps you could organise something to help others.

2. Find out more about the current situation in Afghanistan. What could you do to help the people there? Design an illustrated leaflet to encourage people to help Afghans in need.

# Marking life's stages

# 6  Birth smoking ceremony

Far out in the wilderness of the bush, with few trees and dusty desert all around, the mother – or it may be the grandmother – gathers the special bark from trees and cradles it in her arms. A small pit in the ground has been dug and the bark is placed inside it. Wood and leaves are added to make a small pile. Then it is all lit and the fire takes hold, flaring at first, then smouldering and giving off sweet smoke.

A baby is brought forward and handed to the woman crouching at the fire pit… She takes the baby and holds it over the smoking embers and all those around watch expectantly. The smoke wraps itself around the baby and tears flow from its eyes, wrenched out by the smoke. The mother too has flowing tears, which may be from the smoke or caused by the emotion of the ritual – a moment shared

between her and the child which has been shared by mothers and their children for as long as anyone can remember – and it may happen again at other times in this child's life.

The baby is moved back and forth through the swirling smoke. Sometimes it is barely visible as it disappears into the smoky tendrils coming from the earthy pit. The mother may sing sweetly or hum quietly, words may be said, or silence may prevail. The women watching may be remembering other times when the smoking has been carried out – perhaps with their own children, or those of others before them. Each knows that she is part of something bigger, something older, something which has taken place for thousands of years… and something which is part of who they are as a people.

Soon the ceremony is over and the smoke dies away. The blackened bark, now turned to charcoal, may be wiped over the baby as protection against many different things. Some say that the smoking is to make the child strong and healthy. Some say it keeps bad things away from the child. Some say it heals. Others do not know what it is for, only that it has always been done and so to no longer do it would be wrong…

## Marking birth

**Talking and listening**

- This ceremony takes place amongst Aboriginal peoples in Australia. What do you already know about Aboriginal beliefs?
- Why do you think only women are present at this ceremony?
- Some women may not know what this ceremony is about – should you know what something means before you take part in it?
- The ceremony is 'part of who they are'. What do you think this means?
- What ceremonies do you know of that are linked to birth and the early life of a baby?

Birth is a very significant step in your life – and can still be quite a dangerous process for mother and child, even in the modern world. Many human societies and belief systems have ways of marking the safe delivery of a baby into the world. In some, these are about welcoming the baby into the community. In others, they are about protecting the baby from harm and ensuring that its life starts off in the best possible way.

In some places events linked to birth involve only women – they are not seen as fit for men. In other cultures ceremonies marking the birth of a baby may involve only men – they are not seen as fit for women!

A baby is an addition to the family, a reminder that life is constantly changing and moving on and a symbol of the new eventually replacing the old. Babies are considered to be both a gift and a responsibility and of value not only to individual families, but to wider communities too. This is why, wherever you go in the world, you're likely to find some kind of event which marks the birth of a baby and welcomes it into the human family – a family which has existed for millions of years.

Perhaps your own birth was marked in some way – perhaps it was celebrated by your family and your community. Perhaps, one day, you too will mark the birth of your own child with something special.

## Active Learning

1. In what different ways is the birth of a baby marked around the world? You could look at some of the ceremonies carried out by the major religions of the world such as:
   - Christenings in Christianity
   - circumcision in Judaism
   - the shaving of the baby's hair in Islam
   - the Naamkaran in Hinduism
   - a Humanist naming ceremony.
   You could work in groups to look at one in detail and display your findings.

2. Imagine you had to write some words to say at a ceremony welcoming a baby into the world. What would you say? Write a short speech which you might give.

3. Think about all the people who are affected by the birth of a baby and what this baby means for them. For each one, discuss what the joys of having a new addition to the family or community would be, and also what fears families and communities might have about the future life of a new child.

4. In many communities and cultures of the world, carrying out traditions (such as the smoking ceremony) is thought to be very important – even if people don't always know why! What traditions are there in your country/culture which people still follow? Do they always know why? Find out about local traditions and ceremonies where you live. When did they begin and what is their purpose?

## Progress Check

1. Answer these questions about the smoking ceremony:
   a. Where do smoking ceremonies generally take place?
   b. Who attends and why do you think this is the case?
   c. How is the fire pit constructed?
   d. What happens to the baby during the ceremony?
   e. What is usually done at the end of the ceremony?
   f. What do people think the main purposes of the ceremony are?
   g. Why do you think no men are present at the ceremony?

2. Design an illustrated information leaflet about the smoking ceremony.

3. Write out eight sentences about the smoking ceremony, put them in the wrong order and pass to someone else to rewrite in the correct order.

## On your own

1. The smoking ceremony is often closely linked to the Aboriginal beliefs about the importance of dreaming. Find out more about this and why it is important in the lives of Aboriginal peoples.

2. Choose one other ceremony which marks the birth of a child and find out more about what is done and why. You should choose a different event to the one you may have covered in the activities above.

It wasn't only a day of excitement for Caitlin – it was a day of celebration for the whole family. She had been preparing for many months. Some of this had been in school time and some in a small group on a Sunday, run by Father Michael. She had learned the catechism – though she found it tricky to spell. But she knew what it meant, more or less anyway.

She had also been with her mum to buy the dress. Despite being only seven, the dress was like a bride's dress – all in white, with metres of fine material which bunched out to the side, making her feel like she should be on top of the Christmas tree. She also had a head-dress of the same white material with tiny twinkling pearls and spangled sequins to catch the light and dazzle all around.

Caitlin knows that she is taking part in an event which her parents also did and her grandparents too – all the way back through her family history. She's been told that the whole thing is what the Church calls 'a mystery', and she's still not quite certain about it. Something to do with the small piece of bread that she eats – except it's more like a thin wafer – being the body of Jesus, and the wine she sips being his blood. Maybe she'll understand it a bit more once she's been through it.

Once she's done this she's grown up a little bit more and will have to attend church every Sunday, which will probably be quite hard because she enjoys sleeping more than getting up. After the event, there's going to be a big party with loads of her family there to celebrate her first communion. She'll be getting some presents too. Perhaps a wee white Bible with silver lettering on the front, or a rosary made of shiny beads. But she's also hoping – not so secretly – that she'll be getting some nice new jewellery too.

## Talking and listening

- Have you had a first communion – or do you know of anyone who has?
- First communion, or Eucharist, is an important Christian celebration – what do you know about it?
- Caitlin was dressed in what looked like a mini wedding dress. Why do you think this was?
- At first communion, you make a commitment to becoming a member of the Roman Catholic Church. Do you think seven years old is too young to be doing this?
- Some Roman Catholics recognise that seven-year-olds are just children and believe that their family 'makes the commitment for them'. What do you think they mean by this?

## First communion in the Roman Catholic faith

Communion is known as a sacrament in the Roman Catholic Church, and first communion marks your entry into full membership of the faith. Here, you commit yourself not only to attending church, but also to living your life according to the teachings of Christianity in the Roman Catholic tradition. This will involve things such as prayer, helping others and following a set of moral rules.

First communion is an important event in the life of a Roman Catholic and in the lives of his or her family. It is a way of expressing your beliefs publicly, as well as maintaining a tradition which has been around for a long time. In Scotland, many Roman Catholics see events such as this as ways of expressing their identity and culture as well as a religious act. Roman Catholics were a minority group in Scotland for a long time and, when you're in the minority, keeping your identity strong through the practising of your traditions can take on extra importance.

Children are a vital part of maintaining your identity – because they will take the traditions of the faith into the future and safeguard them for generations to come. So, for Roman Catholics, traditions such as first communion are a way to make sure that their faith – and way of life – survives for many years to come. The fact that the child is only seven isn't important because the commitment is also made by their family on their behalf, and this helps keep families strong.

### Active Learning

1. Find out more about the activities which take place prior to and during a first communion. Make up a Q&A sheet for parents and children which explains what first communion is and why it happens.

2. Items associated with first communion can be very elaborate. Look up some websites and describe the kinds of things which are available for first communions (try www.firstholycommunion.co.uk). You could also work out how much a typical first communion is likely to cost a family.

3. First communion is one of the seven sacraments of the Roman Catholic Church. Find out what the others are and what they involve. Display your findings.

4. What evidence is there of the existence of the Roman Catholic faith in your community? Find a map of your local area and mark on it any evidence of the Roman Catholic faith. You could mark out churches, schools and historically or culturally significant places.

## On your own

1.  There has often been tension in Scotland between the Roman Catholic community and the Protestant community, which may be linked to sectarian conflict. Find out more about this and about how organisations in Scotland today try to challenge sectarianism. For example, see www.ltscotland.org.uk/supportinglearners/ positivelearningenvironments/inclusionandequality/ challengingsectarianism/index.asp

2.  In what ways are children welcomed into the community where you live? Are there any special ceremonies or events to mark changes throughout childhood? Carry out your own research into this and create a presentation of your findings.

### Progress Check

1.  Answer these questions about first communion:
    a.  At what age does this take place? Do you think this is too young? Explain your answer.
    b.  What must the child do at first communion?
    c.  In what different ways might a family/community mark first communion?
    d.  What does first communion commit a person to?
    e.  What parts of first communion are 'religious' and what parts are 'cultural'?
    f.  How do events such as these keep traditions alive?

2.  How 'free to choose' do you think children are about whether or not they take first communion? What issues might this raise? Is it important for adults to guide children towards following practices such as this?

3.  Write an invitation card for a first communion explaining what the event is about.

I had never been outside the community before then – at least not without my parents. I had been born and brought up there with my family all around me all the time. I grew up with my neighbours and we shared everything, and we passed through life together, the good times and the bad.

And then, of course, I became a teenager. The parents I had looked up to for so long became people who were alien to me. I began to notice their faults more than their good points and I challenged everything they said – even the way of life they had chosen and chosen for me. And so, like others, I left and went out into the real world. At least that's what I thought it was.

I didn't become a completely different person though – as some of my friends did. I could have tried drugs and sex but I didn't. I did try alcohol, and it wasn't as terrible as I thought it would be, but nor was it so special either. I danced, I partied,

I wore things which I never imagined I would wear in public – I even swore. I didn't bother with religion at this time and tried to do everything I could to forget the simple and slightly embarrassing ways of my parents.

Many of my friends were captivated by the outside world – or trapped by it if you prefer to think of it that way. I enjoyed many things but – to my surprise – it didn't really satisfy me. I thought some of the activities were pointless and empty, some were disrespectful of others and some were, well, downright dangerous. I could have stayed out there for the rest of my life. Some do – though they are shunned by their families. But I decided to return to my home where I would commit myself to stay and accept the ways in which I had been brought up.

I have a daughter now who will soon have to make the same choices. I don't know whether she will choose to leave or to return – but I do know that it will be her choice. I hope she makes the right one.

# Making adult choices

The Amish are a group of Christians who moved to the USA from Europe a few hundred years ago. They live in tightly knit communities where they have as little contact with the outside world as possible. Generally they do not use machinery and live a simple life based on the teachings of the Bible. They dress in plain clothes which appear to others as old-fashioned, and have very strict rules about behaviour.

However, when an Amish teenager reaches a certain age, he or she may go through the process known as Rumspringa. At this point in their lives, the teenager has to choose between a continued life in the community and a life outside it where no further contact with the community will be permitted.

If, after Rumspringa, the teenager chooses not to remain part of the community then they will be shunned by its members – their community will no longer have anything to do with them. If they choose to remain in the community then they will be baptised, become full adult members, and remain there for the rest of their lives following the Amish way of life.

Many teenagers on Rumspringa stay in the community but just behave in ways which are not normal within the community. Others leave and try out life in the USA (or the 'English world' as the Amish often call it). They dress and behave like ordinary American teenagers and are permitted to try out anything they like. Interestingly, most choose to return and take their place in the community in which they were brought up – turning their backs on the modern world and all that it offers.

## Active Learning

1. Rumspringa happens in Mennonite communities too. Find out where these communities came from and where they are now. Why did they leave those countries and why did they settle where they have? How do they dress and why do they live their lives the way they do? Prepare a display or a mini project about your findings.

2. Discuss the kinds of things teenagers commonly get up to in the modern world. Are they more 'badly behaved' than previous generations? Why do teenagers and their parents often have trouble getting on with each other?

3. Imagine an Amish teenager spent a week living with you. What differences between their life and yours do you think they would find? Write a diary entry that an Amish teenager might write after spending a week with you and your friends.

4. Amish communities believe that many things about the modern world are not as attractive as we like to think they are. For each of the following, think about why the Amish might find that they make life worse instead of better:
   a. mobile phones
   b. the Internet
   c. cars
   d. TV and computer games
   e. eating your dinner while watching TV
   f. shopping.

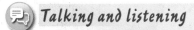
## Talking and listening

- What are the good and bad things about being a teenager?
- Do all teenagers fall out with their parents?
- How do you get on with your parents? How has this changed as you've got older?
- What things about the world might be 'dangerous' or 'disrespectful of others'?
- What do your parents allow you to do and what things do they tell you not to do?

1. Answer these questions about the Amish and Rumspringa:
   a. What happens at Rumspringa?
   b. Where do the Amish live and why?
   c. What things do the Amish not do in their lives and why?
   d. What does 'shunned' mean?
   e. What choice does an Amish teenager have to make?
   f. What choice do most Amish teenagers make and why do you think this is?
   g. What must an Amish teenager do if he or she chooses to return to the community?

2. Some argue that the 'choice' given to the Amish teenager isn't really a fair one because if they do not return they will no longer be able to have anything to do with the community (shunning). Do you think it is a real choice or not?

3. Write a letter from an Amish mother to her daughter who is in the 'English world' where the mother expresses the hope that her daughter will return to the community.

 *On your own*

1. Channel 4 produced a documentary called *The World's Squarest Teenagers* where some Amish teenagers came to live with British families. You should be able to find this on the Internet (for example, on 4 on Demand or YouTube). Watch it and discuss it with others. You could write a review of the programme if you like.

2. Find out more about the lifestyle of Amish and similar communities around the world. Do you think they are right to keep away from the outside world?

Of course I had met my husband before we married – that's pretty normal these days. We met quite a few times actually and he's not bad-looking at all. But yes, our marriage was arranged by both our families – we didn't meet and fall in love and all that stuff some people seem to think is so important. And yes, before you ask, I could have said no to the match. If me and my husband hadn't clicked then I could have rejected him (and he could have rejected me). Neither of our parents would have forced the relationship on us – they know that doesn't make sense.

We all like to think we're so grown up about relationships, but our parents have far more experience of life than we do and a far better understanding of what will work out and what won't. Both families got together and matched us up. They thought about our education, our interests, our caste, our plans for the future – they even consulted our horoscopes. This means that when we were married we were as perfectly matched as any two people can ever be. And our families were matched too, so we had their support right from the start.

I know you think that people should marry 'for love' – but what does that mean really? Sometimes people meet in some very odd places, like noisy nightclubs where everyone's drunk (or worse), you can't hear yourself think, and the people aren't behaving like their real selves at all. When you meet someone in that kind of situation is it anything more than physical attraction? Maybe you just fancy the person – or you're flattered by the fact that they seem to fancy you. But you might find that, when this physical attraction wears off, you have nothing in common – nothing to speak about, no interests that you both share. So, is that love or something else completely?

So did I love my husband when I married him? That's hard to say. But I can say that love has grown in our relationship and is definitely there now. We've been together for many years, and it looks like we're going to stay that way. Plenty of people who get married after 'falling in love' don't stay together for very long and plenty of people whose marriages are arranged do – so don't be too quick to judge the way my marriage began.

## Talking and listening

- What do you know about arranged marriages?
- Should someone's parents be able to 'choose' their wife or husband?
- What does being 'in love' mean?
- How do you think most married couples met?
- Is physical attraction the only important thing in finding a partner for life?

# Arranged marriage in the Hindu community

In many Hindu communities arranged marriages still take place, even in Scotland. The families select the bride and groom based on a very careful analysis of the similarities between the individuals and their families. They match up people whose educational, social and caste backgrounds are similar and who have interests and beliefs in common. They may even consult astrologers who will read the stars to see if the couple is suited. The marriage of two people is seen as a joining together of two families, which is better where the families are not 'mismatched'.

Hindus may argue that love will grow as the relationship develops and that what passes for love in Western marriages is sometimes not love at all, just physical attraction. In most modern Hindu families both prospective partners will be given the option to reject their parents' choice. If they were not allowed this choice then this would be not an arranged marriage but a forced one, and would be contrary to the United Nations Declaration of Human Rights and most countries' laws.

Most modern Hindus believe that it is important to get a marriage right – not only for society now, but also for your spiritual development in this life and in your lives to come. For Hindus, marriage is a sacred relationship which is part of your dharma duty in life. It is therefore more than a choice, it is a responsibility. Upholding the practice of marriage keeps society strong and stable, and is good both for individuals and for families. For many Hindus, the arranged marriage is a way to make sure that the relationship has the best possible chance of surviving throughout this life and beyond.

**Progress Check**

1. Answer these questions about arranged marriages:
   a. In Hinduism, who arranges marriages?
   b. What is taken into account when matching up two prospective partners?
   c. Does the couple get any choice in the matter?
   d. What is the difference between an arranged and a forced marriage?
   e. What does it mean to say that marriage is part of your dharma?
   f. Is marriage in Hinduism for this life only?
   g. In what way is marriage seen as valuable in the Hindu community?

2. 'Sometimes what seems to be love at the start of a relationship is not love at all.' Discuss this statement and explain what it means. What are your views on this?

3. List the things taken into account in arranging a marriage between two people. Now order them according to which ones you think are most to least important and see if you can agree on an order in a group.

## Active Learning

1. If your parents were to choose your husband or wife, what kind of things do you think they would take into account? Now draw up your own list of things you would want them to think about. How similar are the two lists?

2. Have a debate in your class which explores whether marriages should be arranged or based on 'love'.

3. Try a 'matching game' in your class between boys and girls. Write down your favourite foods, music, star sign, where you live, what subjects you're good at in school and so on. Now put these together in class and see who you match up with! Remember to be sensitive towards others. (You might want to make these anonymous.)

4. Devise an anonymous questionnaire which you can hand out to your class's parents. You could ask them questions such as how they met and how similar their interests and background, etc. were/are. Again, be sensitive about how you do this. What do your answers tell you about the ways in which most modern couples meet and about how important having similar beliefs and values is?

## On your own

1. A Hindu wedding is a very elaborate event which involves a long ceremony and many customs leading up to the wedding. Find out more about what happens at a Hindu wedding and report your findings in a way of your choosing.

2. In India, arranged marriages are much more common in rural areas than in towns and cities. Why is this usually the case? Find out about the different lifestyles which rural and city-dwelling people in India are likely to experience.

# A Humanist funeral

'On behalf of Mike's family, I'd like to thank you for coming along today as we remember and celebrate his life. Mike was a loving dad and granddad, and he took great pleasure in bringing happiness to his family. He never showed a great deal of outward emotion, but his children and grandchildren always knew that they were the centre of his life. His love for them was quiet but never wavered – even when life for him became difficult at times, as the pressures of his working life occasionally took their toll.

His work colleagues will always remember him as someone who, even at the most difficult times, would shrug, smile and say "that's what the job is… you just have to get on with it". And his conscientiousness and attention to detail were legendary – a model which others admired and many tried to follow.

At home, one of Mike's hobbies was country music – much to the horror of his wife Louise. She would regularly hide his country music CDs, but eventually resigned herself to it, with the help of two very effective earplugs. She says that it might not have been so bad if Mike hadn't insisted on trying to accompany many of the tunes on his banjo… Louise would suggest that he get some music lessons, to which Mike would always reply that he didn't want to because it might spoil his playing. You may have noticed that country music was playing as you arrived, which Louise chose on Mike's behalf. She said that she would leave the ear plugs out today.

I would like you to join with me in calling up your own memories of Mike: the times you shared with him and the ways in which he made your life just a little better. We remember Mike, and all that he was. And we know that Mike will live on beyond today – in our hearts, in our minds, and in all that he has left behind in the full life that he lived. We express the hope that we each leave the world better than we found it, as Mike did, and that our own contributions in life have enriched the lives of others.'

## Talking and listening

- In what ways are the words said about Mike things you would expect to be said at a funeral?
- Should funerals be sad or joyful events?
- Should people's good points and bad points be mentioned at funerals?
- What would you like said about you at your funeral?
- What music might you like at your funeral?

# Celebrating your only life

Funerals may be sad or joyful events depending on the circumstances of the person's death. They may involve music, singing, poems or other readings. They are almost always likely to involve something being said about the person whose funeral it is. This often only includes the good things about them.

Most funerals involve some kind of religious content, but many funerals in Scotland are now Humanist. These are led by specially trained and licensed Humanists and, according to the Humanist Society of Scotland, are very much on the increase. These funerals are based on the view that this is the only life we get and there is no afterlife such as a heaven. However, we can 'live on' in the memories of those we leave behind and the ways in which we have contributed to the world during our lifetime.

The person in charge of the funeral (celebrant) will discuss with the family of the person who has died how they would like the funeral to be carried out. It may be a very serious and sombre event, or a little lighter, depending upon the wishes of the relatives. Special readings or poems may be said, and family members themselves may speak about their memories of the person who has died. In fact, words written by the person who has died may also be read.

At all times it will be just as respectful as any other kind of funeral, and Humanists say it is a far more appropriate way to say goodbye to someone who has had no connection with religion during his or her life – even if they were not officially a Humanist. Humanist funerals can take place in cemeteries or crematoria just like any other kind of funeral. For Humanists, it is a way of celebrating the only life we will ever have.

**Funerals Without God**

A practical guide to humanist and non-religious funeral ceremonies

Jane Wynne Willson
British Humanist Association

## Active Learning

1. Some people believe that it is good to plan your funeral ahead with your family. That way, your family doesn't have to worry about whether they have made the right choices. They don't see this as morbid but as a sensible thing to do. Think about the kind of funeral you would like. What special requests might you have?

2. Many people write speeches they would like to be read out at their funeral as their way of saying goodbye. Write your own speech.

3. Archaeological discoveries show us that, right from the earliest humans, disposing of the dead has been done in ways which have expressed beliefs and views about the meaning of life (and the possibility of an afterlife).  For example, burying people with special objects (or even sacrificing people to be buried alongside them). Find out more about the different ways in which people have been buried throughout history and display your findings.

4. Local graveyards can tell you a lot about the beliefs people have about death and what it means. If you can visit a local graveyard, write about what the memorials and headstones say. You should seek permission for this first and always remember to behave respectfully when in the graveyard. You can also find examples of memorials and gravestones on the Internet.

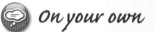

### Progress Check

1. Discuss these statements about funerals and write down any interesting points raised:
   a. Funerals should be celebrations, not gloomy events.
   b. Religion should only be present at a funeral if the person who has died was religious in life.
   c. Funerals should be respectful – there are some things which shouldn't happen at funerals.
   d. At funerals, only good things about the person who has died should be mentioned.

2. The committal of the coffin will take place where it is to be buried or cremated, but a ceremony remembering the dead person can take place anywhere. Humanist events don't usually take place in churches. Discuss places which you think are suitable or unsuitable for such events. Where might you like yours if you were having a Humanist event instead of a religious one?

3. If you were going to have a Humanist funeral, what would you like said about you?

### On your own

1. Find out more about Humanist funerals at www.humanism.org.uk/ceremonies/humanist-funerals-memorials and www.humanism-scotland.org.uk/ceremonies/funerals.html and write a report of your findings.

2. Humanists often argue that people who are not religious have religious funerals because they didn't know that any other choice was possible. Devise a short questionnaire which asks people about the kind of funeral they would like and whether they would like a religious one or not.

# Big questions

3

The funny thing is, I get on quite well with the ghost. I'm never completely sure when he's going to appear, but I kind of feel his presence before I see him. He'll often pass me on the stairs – although his stairs seem to be a bit lower than mine because you can only see him from the knees upwards. Mostly though I don't see him at all, I just hear him moving about. Sometimes it's just a soft bang and other times it's like he's moving the furniture around. Then there are the things that go missing without explanation… but they always reappear somewhere else – he's obviously only borrowing them.

This is an old hotel, but it was built on the site of even older homes, way back in time. None of the guests has ever seen him – and that's probably just as well because that might not be good for business. Mind you, the idea of a haunted hotel probably appeals to some people! And no, before you ask, I didn't make him up to attract ghost-hunting customers. In fact I rarely speak much about him at all. Of all my staff, only one has ever said they think they might have seen him, but they described him a little differently to how he is when I see him. Perhaps he trusts me somehow and that's why he appears only to me.

No, I'm never scared by him, and I've never felt threatened by him. He just seems to fit into the building somehow, and I think I'd actually miss him if he wasn't around. I once had a scientist staying here who asked me if the place was haunted. When we started talking about it, it turned out that he was a parapsychology researcher at Edinburgh University – someone who scientifically investigates supernatural things. He wanted to come back with a whole pile of science gadgets to see if he could record the ghost. He also wanted to test me – maybe he thinks it's all in my head. But I said no because I'm quite comfortable with my ghostly friend and wouldn't like to scare him off.

## Talking and listening

- What do people believe ghosts are?
- Do you believe in ghosts?
- Have you or has anyone you know ever had any experience of what they think might have been a ghost?
- What evidence might you need before you believed in ghosts?
- Do you think people want to believe there are ghosts? Why might this be?

# Belief in ghosts

There are probably only three answers to the question 'Do ghosts exist?' The first is that they do. The second is that some physical or psychological process is mistaken by people as evidence for the existence of ghosts. The third is that ghosts do not exist and what we see or hear is either all in our mind or the result of expectation, suggestion or just plain lies!

Parapsychologists do investigate ghosts and claims of the supernatural, but they're just as likely to investigate the mental processes of the person making the claim as to set up infra-red cameras in supposedly haunted houses. Spiritualists are people who claim to contact the spirits of the dead which, in their opinion, can bring comfort to their surviving relatives. Critics of spiritualists argue that what they do is something called 'cold reading' (saying things that are so vague that they're bound to match up with someone in their audience).

Perhaps there is some spiritual dimension to life – unseen things, inexplicable things – or perhaps it's all just some quirk of nature which we haven't found the scientific explanation for yet. However, belief in ghosts exists everywhere – even in our very scientific and technological modern world. Why is this? Perhaps it is because we like to think that there is 'more' to life than meets the eye. Maybe it is because it is somehow comforting to think that our life will go on after our death. Or it could be that we just misunderstand what we see and hear. Or perhaps we just like a good argument!

![Active Learning]

1. There are many TV programmes about ghosts. How do these programmes investigate the claims? What conclusions do they come to? Why have they never produced proof so far which is impossible to refute? Discuss these programmes in class and, if possible, you could watch one and discuss the evidence afterwards, such as www.scottish-paranormal.co.uk

2. How widespread is belief in ghosts? Devise a questionnaire which asks people about their belief in ghosts and explores any stories they may have.

3. Spiritualists claim to get messages 'from the other side' (from the spirits of people who have died). What do you think of their claims? Find out about the claims of such spiritualists and the spiritualist church. You should also investigate what is known as the 'Barnum Effect' and compare this with spiritualism. See www.thespiritualist.org and http://psych.fullerton.edu/mbirnbaum/psych101/barnum_demo.htm

4. On the Internet you will find many photographs which claim to be of ghosts. Make a display of these and get people to write what they think it is on Post-Its. You can then compare the different things that people see and the different beliefs they have about what they see.

1. Answer these questions in relation to the claims of the hotel owner who sees the ghost:
   a. How do you think he might feel the ghost's presence before he sees him? What other explanation could there be for this?
   b. What else could explain the noises and the missing objects?
   c. Is the fact that no guests have ever seen the ghost in any way significant?
   d. Why might some people be attracted to staying in a haunted hotel?
   e. Should the hotel owner let the parapsychologists investigate?
   f. Do you think the evidence in this story points to the existence of a ghost or something else?

2. Debate in class: 'There's no such thing as a ghost.'

3. List five alternative explanations which might be possible when someone claims to have seen a ghost.

## On your own

1. Imagine that your friend claims he has seen a ghost. Write a list of questions you would ask to investigate his claims.

2. In various places in the world there are prizes offered for anyone who successfully proves something supernatural. Find out about this and about why the people who offer this prize have done so. See www.skeptics.com.au/features/prize

Well of course I don't feel things the way you do exactly... But then, now that I think of it, I don't know how you feel things exactly. Nor does anyone else for that matter, I suppose. I do, however, have emotions and can laugh and cry, feel sad and feel love. But I can switch this part of my programming off if I want to. I hear many humans can switch their emotions off too. Even if I say so myself, my memory is pretty amazing. I can remember everything that's ever happened to me, every thought I've had, everything I've ever seen or heard. I believe that's better than any human, because I understand that you can forget things – and that some people can even forget who they are and who their closest relatives are.

I do require regular energy top-ups to keep going though. If I didn't have these then that would be the end of me I guess. But then, without your food and water, you'd not last long either. I have built up many relationships with people (and other robots of course) and some of them depend on me pretty heavily. My human friends tell me that they often completely forget that I'm a robot. Oh, perhaps I didn't mention, I'm not metal with flashing lights or anything – those kind of robots are long

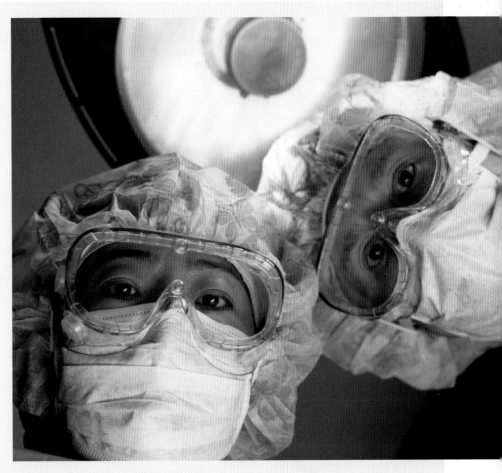

gone. I look exactly like a human being – I have synthetic skin which feels just like real human skin and sweats and everything. And, yes, if you prick me I do indeed bleed.

Because of my incredible ability to learn and never forget, I work as a surgeon (on humans). I have never misdiagnosed anything or ever got any medical procedure wrong. What's more, I never get tired and so never make mistakes. I think any human surgeon would find it impossible to match my record. Oh, and another thing, I

am never able to harm anything. If I even thought about harming anything, then it would trigger my complete shutdown. My human friends think that it would be good if that could happen to humans sometimes too.

However, I am still a robot and I could be switched off by my owners (the hospital) whenever they wanted to. Perhaps one day, when a newer version of my model is built, then they'll switch me off and use that one instead. I hope that day never comes – I enjoy my life.

- Do you think a robot like that will ever be made?
- Would such a robot be almost (or completely) human?
- What would the world be like if such robots existed? Would it worry you that you wouldn't be able to tell the difference between a robot and a human being?
- What do you think the most advanced computers around today can do?
- Could a robot ever replace a human completely?

## The rights of robots

The movies *A.I. Artificial Intelligence*, *I, Robot*, *Bicentennial Man* and *Westworld* as well as many TV programmes such as *Star Trek* and *Battlestar Galactica* all include robotic beings which you wouldn't know were not human. Of course, these are science fiction, but many scientists think that such robots could become reality one day. If this does happen, would such robots be the same as humans, or would they still be machines? Should they have the same right as humans, different rights, or no rights at all? Would it be wise to give them emotions? Would it be wise to make them better than humans at doing certain things?

We give human rights to all humans, and not to other thinking beings. Is this because those other beings are not as intelligent as we are or is it because they do not

understand things the way we do? Or are we just discriminating against other things because they're not human?

Some humans completely lose their memories and can even lose their own sense of self-awareness. Are these people still human? Some humans seem to be capable of great cruelty towards others – almost as if they have no feelings at all. Are such people still human? Some human bodies go into a 'shutdown' mode, which we call a coma or persistent vegetative state (PVS). Is such a person still human?

Generally speaking, we grant all human beings full human rights no matter what their 'condition'. If a robot was in every possible respect like a human being, shouldn't they have rights too?

*Active Learning*

1. In one of the Star Trek films, Commander Data (a very advanced robot) is given a chip which makes him experience emotions just like a human. Captain Picard informs Data that being troubled by our emotions is what makes us human. Discuss this in class and note down what you find. Which of our emotions are the most problematic for us? If we could 'switch them off', should we do so?

2. In many sci-fi movies (such as *The Terminator*) there is a fear that super-able robots would turn on humans. How do you think scientists building robots could avoid that? Write down your thoughts.

3. Are there times when humans are no longer human? (For example, if you lose your memory or are in a coma/PVS). Would it be right to harvest the body organs of such people to donate to those who need them and who have all their human abilities?

4. Often animals are treated very differently to humans because they are not human. What examples of this are there, and is it right for humans to behave towards non-humans in these ways? Prepare a presentation on this issue.

 **Progress Check**

1. Discuss and answer these questions… if you can:
   a. Does anyone know how anyone else actually feels things?
   b. Is a person who has no memory of their life still the same person?
   c. What would be the best uses of near-human robots?
   d. If a robot was like the surgeon robot, should 'he' have human rights?
   e. How much care should scientists take when building robots to avoid them ever coming into conflict with humans?
   f. Should near-human robots ever be built?

2. Debate this in class: 'No matter how advanced a robot was it would never be alive.'

3. Write out five rights you think robots should have.

 *On your own*

1. Watch one of the movies referred to in this section and write up a report about the robot issues raised by the movie. (Make sure the movie is suitable for your age group!)

2. Ask as many people as you can the following question: 'If a robot appeared to be human in every respect, would you want such a robot as part of your family?'

I've lived through all three responses to this question now. When I was younger my family was very religious and, therefore, so was I. But I didn't just follow what they told me – I'm not a sheep! I felt the presence of God in my life, and it also made sense to me. I mean, how else could the Universe have come about other than by being made by some super-powerful being?

I didn't buy the whole evolution thing – it just seemed to make far more sense that God had made everything. I knew that bad things happened in the world. Sometimes I blamed the Devil for this – or just bad people – but mostly I just trusted that God didn't stop them because he had to let us exercise our own freedom… But then I seemed to change my mind about it all.

The more I learned about evolution, the more I didn't think that any God was necessary. Also, I started to feel the presence of God less and less in my life, and the idea of God no longer made sense. I could see that the Universe could just cause itself and, as for the existence of evil, I couldn't blame a Devil any more (too childish). And I wouldn't let God off the hook with some nonsense about letting evil happen to let us make free choices – why couldn't God let us think we were free and stop evil at the same time? I mean, is our freedom more important than the suffering of some innocent child? No, God didn't make any sense to me… and I made sure I told others about that.

Now, at my age, the things you thought you were so sure about you find yourself less sure about. Whether God created the Universe or a Big Bang did – who knows and, quite honestly, who cares? The answer wouldn't change my life. I still don't feel God in my life, but then whether I feel his presence or not has nothing to do with whether he exists or not!

And evil, yes, there's still plenty around – but the more I see it the more I want to hope that there is some kind of God. Perhaps then evil people would have to answer for their actions. And, of course, there's far more good around in the world – we just notice the evil more. Perhaps God isn't all-powerful as I used to think, perhaps he's just doing his best and sometimes he gets it right and other times he doesn't. I know it's not what the priests and ministers might say… but it works for me.

ADAM & ÈVE CHASSÉS DU PARADIS TERRESTRE.

### Talking and listening

- How would you answer the question 'Does God exist?'
- How did you reach that answer?
- What different views are there in your class about this question?
- Does belief in God need evidence?
- If there is a God, should he make his existence obvious?

# God

Theists believe in a God, Atheists do not and Agnostics have not reached a conclusion on this issue. Some think that belief in God is exactly that – a matter of belief. Some think there is evidence for the existence of God and others do not. Some think that the existence of evil in the world proves that there cannot be a God, and others think that evil is just part of the law of nature and human freedom and not much to do with God at all.

Some think there must have been a creator of all, and others think that everything came into being without a creator. Besides which, where would a creator come from if no one made him? Some think that God is male, some female and some think God is a spiritual being. Some think God is 'out there', others that he is 'in here'. Some think God is involved in our everyday lives and others that he is remote and unreachable.

Some think that all these beliefs are silly and that God is just something we have made up to help us cope with life, or that we're kidding ourselves that such a thing exists. Some think that we only believe in God because that's how we've been brought up and that God is an old-fashioned idea and so we should give up this out-of-date notion. Some think that God is no more real than the tooth fairy and others think that God is the most powerful being in the Universe – the source of everything and beyond our human understanding.

Some think that whether there is a God or not is one of the biggest questions you will ever think about, and others think wondering about the existence of God is a pointless exercise because we can never know the answer. Some believe so strongly in God that they will die on his behalf and may even kill others; others think that killing anything is considered to be wrong by God. As you can see, it's a tricky issue.

## Active Learning

1. Carry out a survey into the different beliefs people have about God and report on your findings.

2. Find out about one of the following arguments for the existence of God. Discuss it and explain how well you think it argues for the existence of God and how well people have challenged it:
   a. the argument from design
   b. the first cause argument
   c. the problem of evil.

3. What difference would it make to your life and to the world if there:
   ■ definitely was a God
   ■ definitely was not a God.
   Discuss this in class and prepare a presentation on your findings.

4. Humanists don't believe in God. They had a recent publicity campaign which stated 'There's probably no God, so stop worrying and enjoy your life.' Have a debate in class which explores the issue of whether those who believe in God worry about it or don't enjoy their life.

1. Discuss and answer these questions about the existence of God:
   a. Is there any evidence for or against the existence of God?
   b. Did something have to make the Universe?
   c. Does the existence of evil prove that there's no God?
   d. Do you have to 'feel the presence of God' before you can believe in him?

2. Have a class debate: 'It doesn't matter whether there is a God or not.'

3. How many words linked to the idea of God can you produce using the letters G, O and D at the start of each word?

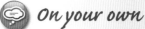 **On your own**

1. The issue of whether there is a God or not is hotly debated around the world. Have a look on the Internet to find out what different views there are and what kinds of disagreements there are about the existence of God.

2. Discuss this question with others and note down their responses: 'What is/would be proof of the existence of God that no one could ever argue with?'

Don't rush to judge me too quickly… you may have done the same if you had been in my position. You see, it had to be done, there was no other choice. I knew it was wrong even as I was doing it, but I couldn't have done things any differently. I thought about it well before the day arrived and have thought about it ever since. Believe me, I wake each morning and the images come into my mind before my eyes have even opened to take in the new day.

There were others like me too – we shared a silence about what was happening. We knew that if we broke that silence, the awfulness of what was taking place around us would finally break through our shaky defences, and we may weaken and step back from what was to come. But then, that would have been the end of us. Most of us could have coped with that, but we knew that our families would be at risk too should we make a different choice… and none of us was prepared to face that possibility.

I know that I am individually responsible for what I did. I accept that and know the responsibility is mine alone. I could try to blame others, but that would simply be a way to hide my own actions, to disguise them as something they were not, and to try to win your sympathy, which I know I cannot have and do not deserve. But we are human – each one of us – and sometimes the situations we find ourselves in leave us feeling trapped, unable to see any way out… except one.

In my case, the only way out was to walk through a fire which would consume me for the rest of my life. But a fire which would take only me – and leave the rest of my family untouched and unaware. What I did, no one will ever call right… but there are many reasons why we do wrong and they are rarely simple ones. Do not pity me nor try to excuse my actions. Simply think more carefully about what, for you, is right.

## Talking and listening

- Where does your sense of right and wrong come from?
- In your opinion, is there anything which is always right or always wrong?
- Can something ever be right and wrong at the same time?
- What kinds of things do you think are right and wrong?
- Does what is right and wrong change according to the situation you find yourself in?

# Right and wrong

What makes something right or wrong has been debated by philosophers for many years. Some think that something is right if what happens after the thing is done (the consequences) are good, and wrong if they're bad. Some think that there are some things which are always right or wrong, no matter where, when or how you live – or what your life is like. Some think we are doing the right thing if we follow the law and the rules of our society – but others think that some of those very rules and laws might be wrong and so we shouldn't follow them. Some get their sense of right and wrong from their beliefs (religious or otherwise) or from their parents or their peers, or maybe even by copying the behaviour of people they see on TV. Some feel that right and wrong can only be decided when you are in a particular situation, and what you think is right or wrong may change if the situation changes. Or perhaps something is only right if it is good for most people – even if it makes a few people very sad.

We all have a basic idea of what we think is right and wrong, and your idea may be very similar to others' or it may be very different. However, if we are to live comfortably alongside other people (and other living things… maybe even robots) we need to have an idea of what we each think is right and wrong.

 *Active Learning*

1. Have a look through a typical daily newspaper. Find examples of issues of right and wrong. Display these in your class and have people in your class write their own views about the situation.

2. Rules about right and wrong are often drawn up in moral codes such as the Ten Commandments, the Eightfold Path and the UN Declaration of Human Rights. Find these – and any other moral codes you can find – and highlight the similarities and differences between them.

3. Our parents, peers and the media can all influence what we think is right and wrong. Discuss in class how these three affect your own view of right and wrong.

4. Ideas of what is right and wrong change over time. Do a timeline for one of the following issues showing how we have changed in how we think about such issues. You can do this in relation to Scotland or to the wider world:
   a. votes for women
   b. the education of working-class people
   c. slavery
   d. the rights of children
   e. the rights of animals.

THIS IS THE PERSON
WHO WAKES UP
EVERY DAY KNOWING
WHAT IS RIGHT
WHAT IS WRONG
IN EVERY INSTANCE
WITH NO GREY AREAS
AND IS SURE OF IT

PUT THEM IN A
PERSPEX BOX
AND PUT THEM
IN THE MUSEUM
SO THAT WE CAN
ALL MARVEL AT THEM

**Progress Check**

1. Discuss and answer these questions, thinking back to the introduction to this chapter:
   a. Would you ever do something wrong to protect yourself?
   b. Would you ever do something wrong to protect others?
   c. Why might people do things which are wrong even when they know they are wrong?
   d. Is it okay to do something wrong if you can say that someone else 'made you do it'?
   e. Is it okay to do something wrong because 'other people are doing it too'?
   f. Is what's right and wrong simple or difficult to work out?

2. Debate in class: 'Every person is individually responsible for their own actions.'

3. Write your own list of things that are right and wrong, but don't identify which is which. Now pass to someone else and get them to put each thing under the headings 'right' or 'wrong'. Is their list the same as yours?

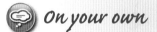
**On your own**

1. Find out about two famous philosophers who had views about right and wrong and make a short factfile about their views: John Stuart Mill and Immanuel Kant. If you have a Higher RMPS class in your school you could ask them to help you with this!

2. Write about the last time you had to choose between right and wrong. What choice did you make and why? You may want to keep this writing to yourself.

John Burbleblott is a genius and he has decided that he wants to live forever. He has developed a very clever computer program. Every evening before heading to bed with a nice cup of cocoa, he uploads every single thing he has seen, heard, felt and experienced that day… everything. Don't ask how he manages to record all that into this program – no one else could possibly understand but John does, and that's all that matters. It's added to everything else he has recorded – his whole lifetime's experiences.

John knows that one day his human body will die but he – John Burbleblott, genius – will live on because everything that he is will be stored in a very large hard drive in a number of computers. When the program which runs this is fully activated, all that is John will come to life in the computer and will think and experience things in exactly the way John always did while in his human body.

Now John's a genius remember, so he knows that being electronic in a computer isn't the same as being human. Of course he's thought of that. You see, he's also very rich, and he has his own team of scientists who have almost completed their building of an entire human body. It isn't made up of spare parts or anything – that would be quite wrong. No, it's a whole new synthetic human body and in every single respect it is completely human – except for one: its brain is empty at the moment.

Now a brain is a bit like a computer, and all its thoughts and experiences are nothing more than little electric currents going this way and that. When the body's ready, all of the thoughts that John has stored in the computer will be downloaded into the empty brain. This brain will then essentially be John's and it will be linked to the new body – the new John. He's decided to upgrade the body a bit (he never really liked his nose anyway) so the new John will look a little different, but he'll still be John. Eventually this body will wear out too, but that's okay because he'll carry on uploading everything to the computer so that he can download it all again when he needs his next body. John will live forever… simple really.

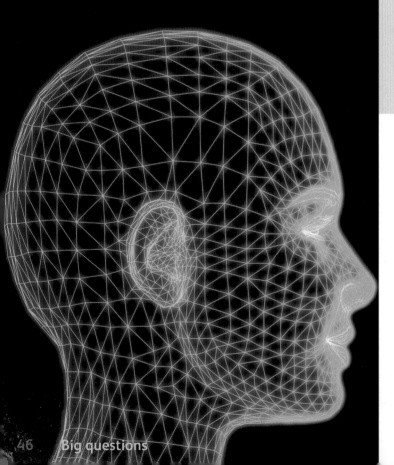

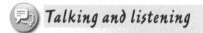 **Talking and listening**

- When 'John' is in the computer, is it John?
- Is the John in the new body still John?
- Do you think uploading yourself into a computer would ever be possible?
- Would you want 'you' to exist in a computer?
- Do you need your body to be you?

# Body, mind, brain, you

Long before there were computers, people wondered about what makes you 'you' and no one else. Was it your mind that made you the person you are – and, if it was, where was this mind? Did you have an eternal soul which inhabited a physical body? In which case, was this 'soul' a part of your body or not, and could this soul exist without being attached to your body? Were you only you if you could recognise yourself – or if you could call up your memories?

And when your memories started to fail you, was that no longer you?

As well as all this confusion about you, there was the tricky issue of how much you changed over the years… Was the old wrinkly you at eighty exactly the same you as the fresh young eighteen-year-old you? And, what's more, was the you at the end of a single day the same you as the one which started it in every way?

Then, of course, science came along and started talking about your brain and DNA and things like that. Had science found the answer to what makes you you? Not quite. What if you could be cloned and an identical you was made from your DNA – would that be you? Or what if your brain could be transplanted into a robot body… would that still be you?

Psychologists can't agree about what your personality is either – but they're quite sure that it can change completely during your life and turn what was you into someone else entirely… So, do **you** know who you are or could you not be you at all?

## Active Learning

1. Discuss and note down how you have changed over the years, physically and mentally. You could plot this with photos of yourself through the years. You could also do this for a week and consider how your thinking has changed and how you have added new memories and lost old ones. In what way is the thing which is you still you?

2. This problem is covered very cleverly by a 'thought experiment' called 'the much-darned sock'. This is about a green woolly sock which, as it wears out over the years, is continually repaired (darned… ask your granny) with red wool. Eventually the green sock is completely red. Is it the same sock? Design an illustrated version of this story which gets people thinking!

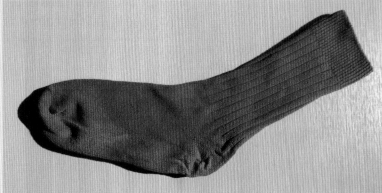

3. Buddhists agree that you don't exist(!). They say that what is you is ever-changing, the endless result of changes to the five skandhas. These skandhas are what make you the person you are – moment by moment. Find out what these are and discuss them. Now explain whether you think these skandhas are or aren't 'you'.

4. Other religions believe in the existence of a soul. Find out about their beliefs in the soul and compare the different beliefs. What do you think?

1. Read about John Burbleblott again and then try to answer these questions:
   a. If you were going to record everything that was you in one day, what would you need to record?
   b. Is John wise to trust himself to the memory of a computer?
   c. Is John wise to want to live forever?
   d. In what ways is a human brain like and not like a computer?
   e. John could download his mind into a woman's body – would that still be John?
   f. If you could, would you copy John?

2. Debate this: 'If it ever became possible to do what John is planning, should the world's governments make it illegal?'

3. Describe the state of your five skandhas today… then do the same tomorrow. Are there any differences?

## On your own

1. What if John in the computer could be downloaded into more than one body; would this be right? Discuss with your parents or friends.

2. Are you ever aware of being aware of yourself? Does this mean that there's another you inside you, watching you? Discuss this and see if you can come to any conclusions.

4

# Environmental issues

Okay, I'm a gorilla. No, not the type who goes clubbing with a beer belly and thinks he's good looking… I'm a real gorilla. I live in the tropical rainforests and, yes, although it may come as a surprise to you… I can think. The trouble is, I can't communicate – not to you people anyway, though I'm not sure you'd listen even if I could.

My whole group is under threat… and so are many of the other beings we share the forests with. Yes, we talk to each other. We have to because there's so little room for us now that we're practically living on top of each other half the time. It's made some creatures pretty grumpy I can tell you. Despite our size and strength we're all vegetarians in the gorilla-world, which is just as well because otherwise we might be eating those we have minor disagreements with. We might have to eventually anyway, as the land which provides our food is getting smaller and smaller each month.

You see, you humans just waltz right into our homes and take what you want… trees mainly, for your paper and your furniture. Never mind that this is our home and has been for generations. I have even heard that you've killed my own kind just because they were in your way, or because you wanted to turn them into some kind of souvenir for sale. Surely no living thing would do that to another living thing? We certainly wouldn't.

We really just want to live our lives in peace and wander around the forests enjoying our home. And we don't really understand why you seem to feel the need to destroy everything of value to us… Is there no other way to meet your needs? This forest used to stretch to the end of the world – now I walk from one end to the other in just a few days. It's a very beautiful forest too. Well it used to be. And there are probably things in this forest that you don't even know exist – and which might be of more use to you than something you can make a chair out of. If there were some way to tell you that what you're doing is wrong, I'd do everything in my power to find it… but like I said, would you listen?

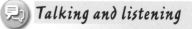 *Talking and listening*

- If animals could talk, what kinds of things might they say?
- Would humans listen to the things animals said?
- Gorillas are 'endangered' – what is an endangered species?
- What kinds of things do humans do which destroy natural habitats?
- How would you feel if someone destroyed your home for their own benefit?

# Can nature have rights?

It's fairly certain that if someone threatened where you live you would complain about it. You might even fight back, and it is likely that others would stand up for you if you were unable to stand up for yourself. And yet, every day, huge areas of natural habitat are destroyed by humans for our own use. It might be to create land for farming, or to make use of the resources there. How much do we care about the rights of the living things that are affected by such activities? Do we care at all?

Obviously animals cannot communicate to us that they'd rather we didn't destroy the places in which they live. So perhaps we have to think for them and ask ourselves how we would feel if we were in their position. Many people believe that nature has rights, just like anything else. In fact, maybe nature has even more rights because it is unable to speak up for itself, and so we have to be extra careful how we treat it.

Perhaps we need to think about how we treat the natural world, because of the possible consequences our actions could have for all life on Earth. For example, if we destroy the world's rainforests, who can say how this might harm the global climate…? Does nature have rights? Do you protect those rights? Perhaps we should be thinking about it…

## Active Learning

1. What areas of the world are under threat from human activities? What are we doing and why? Who or what is harmed by this? On a world map, plot places which are under threat and write about the threats they face.

2. Many animals in the world today are endangered. Find out which ones are most at risk and why. Produce information sheets about one or more – perhaps you could think about adopting one!

3. The world's religions have different views about how humans and nature are linked. Choose two of the world's religions and write about how they value nature. (You could, for example, look at the concept of 'stewardship'.)

4. The rights of nature could be under attack much closer to home. Is there any natural feature near you which is threatened? You could take some photos of this and start up a campaign to protect it!

 ## On your own

1. Visit the website of one organisation which is concerned with the rights of nature such as www. worldwildlife.org Report on one view they have and one way in which they try to protect nature.

2. Create your own set of images about the ways in which the natural world is treated/mistreated by humans. You could set this to appropriate music if you like and perhaps do it as a PowerPoint presentation.

 ### Progress Check

1. Answer these questions in relation to the gorilla story and what you have learned so far:
   a. Why can't gorillas express their anger at how humans are treating their homes?
   b. How does destruction of natural habitats put pressure on the things which live there?
   c. What kinds of things are humans likely to destroy tropical rainforests for?
   d. What kinds of things might be 'of use' to humans in rainforests which we don't even know exist yet?
   e. What could the consequences of destroying the rainforests be?
   f. What is an endangered species?

2. In class you should debate the following: 'Does nature have rights?'

3. Write out five rules for looking after a gorilla's natural habitat.

Only a hundred of us were chosen. There was only one spacecraft which was capable of leaving Earth, never to return. I am the last of that chosen hundred… all the others now on board were born on this ship… Only I have stood on our home planet, some fifty years ago now.

It started with the weather… strange and dramatic changes: snow in the Sahara desert, floods in the Australian outback, storms in Scotland only usually seen in the tropics. Then the land itself seemed to give up. The cycles of crop growth seemed to go haywire and then, finally, things stopped growing altogether. It was as if the land had simply been exhausted by our use of it.

Our population grew and grew and we needed more land to live… but this meant less land to farm so we had to work it harder, until it could produce no more. So we started to eat more wild foods, things we'd never considered before. But this changed our landscape too, and affected the other lives which depended upon

it all. Even in great cities we were hunting wild animals because we could no longer feed agricultural livestock. We could barely feed ourselves.

The world became a tense place… conflicts broke out between nations in their desperate attempts to feed their own people, often at the expense of their neighbours. As war took up our time and energy, so

finding solutions for our hunger were abandoned. Beautiful green places, rich sources of what nourishment was left, were turned barren and empty by our own senseless actions.

And so, in secret, the world's leaders put aside their differences and worked together to send one hundred human beings out into the depths of space – a modern ark – to find a new home and start again. We haven't found that home yet, we are still searching. We are far from Earth now and we were only able to communicate with home for the first few years of our journey. We will never know what became of the Earth, and they will never know what became of us…

### 🗪 Talking and listening

- What examples of 'weird weather' have you heard about recently?
- What do you know about climate change?
- What is the current population of Earth and what is it predicted to be in future?
- Do you think that humans put too much pressure on the land to produce what they need to survive?
- Could our food ever run out?

# The land and life

As human population increases, so too does the stress we put the land under. We need to use more land that scientists call 'marginal'. This is land which isn't really best for growing things, but can be helped to do so by using lots of chemical fertilisers, pesticides and so on. This method produces crops, but there is a serious environmental cost. And, as the land is used more intensively, it takes longer to recover so that it can be used again. Perhaps there could come a point where it is quite simply exhausted and able to produce no more.

One way to try to deal with this is by genetically modifying crops to make them more likely to survive. But this has problems too. Such crops could end up being more likely to get diseases and die out in large numbers… we just don't know.

As well as crops, humans use the land for all sorts of things: wood for paper, grazing for animals, mining for mineral resources and so on. As we use up the land, we have to wonder just how much it can take. And it's not just humans… all living things depend upon what the Earth provides for life.

The more things change, the more at risk life on Earth becomes. Already, many scientists say that our treatment of the land is contributing to climate change. And that climate change could quite possibly lead to major changes on our planet… This could mean the end of life as we know it, and certainly a possible end to human life. Perhaps we should be more careful about how we treat the land. At the moment, Earth is the only home we have.

## Active Learning

1. Just how much of our planet is suitable for growing food crops? On a world map, mark the areas that are currently available for food production and those that are not (because they are populated or unsuitable for growing crops). You could also do the same activity for Scotland. Is there as much space for growing crops as you thought, or is it just that we don't use it?

2. When many of your grandparents were children, it was probably quite likely that they grew food in their own back gardens. As a class, carry out a survey amongst older people in your community. Find out how common this was and compare your findings with how much this goes on nowadays. (You could also discuss the 'Dig for Victory' campaign with your History teachers.)

3. Many people argue that feeding animals which we then eat is bad for the environment because it is wasteful. Find out about the arguments here and explain whether you think meat-eating is bad for the land or not.

4. Many groups are very concerned about environmental issues and campaign to make people more aware. Look this up on the Internet and prepare a presentation about your findings. You could look at a religious group (such as Christian Ecology Link at www.christian-ecology.org.uk) and a non-religious group (such as Friends of the Earth at www.foe.co.uk).

## Progress Check

1. Discuss and answer these questions based on your work in this chapter:
   a. Is the land under threat from human activities?
   b. How have human population levels changed over time?
   c. What is intensive agriculture?
   d. Is raising animals for food a good use of the land?
   e. How might climate change be linked to human activities?
   f. In what ways could (do) food supply issues lead to conflict between people in the world?

2. Should people change their eating habits to help the environment? How could they? Discuss this in class.

3. List five ways in which you could help nature.

## On your own

1. Find out more about genetically modified (GM) foods. Could they be a solution to keeping the world fed?

2. Many people who buy their foods in supermarkets have no real idea about how hard a job farming is – some barely even know how foods are produced. Perhaps you could try to grow something simple that you eat (like a tomato plant), which may help you to understand the timescales involved in food production.

*Rab and Donnie are two Glaswegians on holiday in Edinburgh. They're staying in a nice hotel on Easter Road, though Rab doesn't know why people are looking so oddly at him – he's bought a Hearts football top as a souvenir and he thought wearing it in Edinburgh would please the locals. We join them in the queue at the local chip shop where Rab's just about to place his order…*

**Rab:** Hullawrerrhowzitgaundoll…

**Donnie:** Rab, it's Edinburgh, they'll no' ken whit yer sayin'.

**Rab:** Aye, right enough therr Donnie. Beg yir pardon hen… may I partake of mackerel and chips please?

**Chip-shop woman:** We dinny do mackerel.

**Rab:** Oh well then, I shall instead have the coley and chips.

**Chip-shop woman:** Nae coley either.

**Rab:** Very well… Dab and chips please.

**Chip-shop woman:** It's haddock or cod… Come on… there's a queue.

**Donnie:** Rab, whit ur ye daein' noo? Dab? Coley? Mackerel and chips? Is this sumthin' you've read in a mag aboot Edinburgh, or ur ye just oan the wind-up wi' the locals?

**Rab:** Naw, ah'm no'. Ah watched that Jamie Oliver oan the telly telling us aw aboot how we hud tae change oor ways aboot the fish we eat cos we're killin' the seas. He said we huv tae stoap wi' the haddock and cod…

**Donnie:** Aye, ye'll mibbee get away wi' that in some posh Edinburgh deli, but no in this fine Hibee chip shop establishment.

**Rab:** Naw? Whit dae ye mean Hibee – is that a kind a fish?

**Donnie:** Naw… They dae haddock and cod. That's whit they've goat, so that's whit ye order. They're no likely tae nip doon tae Leith and sling a hook intae the watter tae try and nab some exotic marine creature just cos some idiot weegie wi' a jambo's top on asks fur it ur they?

**Rab:** Nae coley then?

**Donnie:** Naw, nae coley. Noo, get yir order in, ye're drawing attention tae yersel'… again.

**Rab:** Fine, Ah'll just huv a deep-fried creme egg then.

**Donnie:** Aw naw… here we go again…

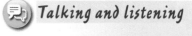

## Talking and listening

- If you're having fish and chips, do you know what kind of fish you're having?
- Things like fish fingers contain fish (unsurprisingly). Do you know what kind of fish they contain?
- If you eat fish, how often do you eat farmed or wild fish?
- How are most fish caught?
- Do you think humans put pressure on the world's oceans?

# The oceans and life

If you approached Earth from space you'd soon realise that most of our planet is actually sea. Much of what humans eat around the world comes from the sea and we eat plenty of types of seafood. However, this appetite has an environmental cost. Many species of sea life are under threat – partly because we are eating them to extinction, but also because of the effects our human activities have on the oceans more generally.

In the waters around our own country, great trawlers drag nets across the sea floor, scooping up all in their path. Much of what is caught is thrown back because people don't want to eat it, or because fishermen are only allowed to catch so many fish. Most of the fish we eat in Scotland are haddock and cod, and these are now under severe threat. Some people who are concerned about the oceans have tried to persuade us to eat a wider range of fish species such as dab, coley and mackerel. But it's not just over-fishing that can harm the oceans: pollution from land often finds its way into the seas, and oil spills take their toll. As well as the plundering of the oceans for other resources which humans require.

Now, the oceans can seem irrelevant if you don't live near them (though most people in Scotland don't live far from the seas), but they are a vital part of the Earth's natural systems. They have a part to play in keeping the climate stable as well as providing food. Ocean currents regulate all sorts of things. In fact, without one ocean current, Scotland would be much colder than it is…

The important thing is that humans can have a very direct and very large effect on the oceans and we don't know what harm this might cause – not just to life in the oceans but to all life on Earth. Perhaps we need to think more carefully about how we treat the oceans.

## Active Learning

1. What kinds of fish do people in your school eat? Do they always know what fish they are eating? Are these foods sustainable? Conduct a questionnaire which explores how much fish is eaten by people in your school, how much they know about where it comes from and the possible environmental impact it has. To help you explore the issues, you could look at www.channel4.com/4food/the-big-fish-fight

2. With the help of your Home Economics department you could prepare some fish recipes using less well-known types of fish. Alternatively, visit your local supermarket and find out what's available at the fish counter. Perhaps you could interview the manager about sustainable fishing practices and how the supermarket supports these (or you could just investigate the food labels on fish products).

3. The world's oceans also play an important part in keeping the climate stable. On a world map, mark the world's ocean currents and show how something that happens in one country might affect others, as well as showing how these currents affect climate.

4. Oil spills can have a serious and immediate effect on ocean life. Find out about one and prepare a display about how this affected the oceans, sea life and the people who depend upon the seas (for example, see www.bbc.co.uk/news/10217739).

**Progress Check**

1. Discuss and answer these questions:
   a. Which fish are most likely to be served up in Scottish chip shops?
   b. Which fish are usually used in products such as fish fingers?
   c. How are most of the fish we eat in Scotland caught?
   d. What are the possible environmental (and human) impacts of over-fishing?
   e. In what other ways are the world's oceans possibly under threat from human activities?

2. Discuss and note down any interesting points: 'In what ways do we depend on the world's oceans?'

3. Carry on the Rab and Donnie conversation where they start talking about other ways in which they could preserve the world's oceans.

*On your own*

1. Visit www.greenpeace.org/international/campaigns/oceans/ and write about three new things you learned about the oceans.

2. In many places in Scotland, fishing was (and still is) a way of life. However, it has seen many changes over the years. Find out about one fishing community and how changes to fishing practices have affected the community.

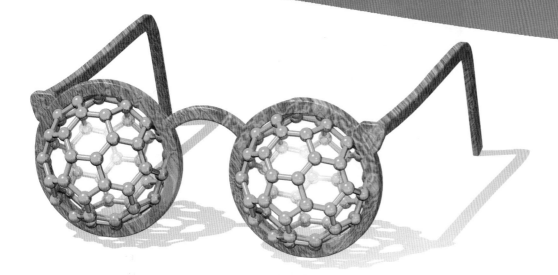

**I am Eric and I am a scientist.** I am interested in how we see the world. I have invented a pair of spectacles which are rather unusual. When you wear them you can see everything that's in the atmosphere. That's radio waves and light waves and sound waves…very pretty patterns. You can also see dust, and little particles of matter, and gases in the atmosphere too – even the carbon dioxide you breathe out… And if you want some fun, wear them while watching a cow! You'll be astounded just how busy your atmosphere is!

**I am Katy and I am a doctor.** I'm looking forward to these spectacles being available. I treat lots of patients with breathing difficulties caused by material in the air, such as pollen. Just imagine how useful these spectacles will be for them. As they're out walking they could dodge little clouds of pollen, or only walk along streets where there are no exhaust fumes from cars.

**I am Ian and I am a gas fitter.** These spectacles will be great. You could see a gas leak right away, which could save your life. You could also see another killer – carbon monoxide. That one's nasty because you can't smell it – but with these spectacles you could see it and deal with it before it deals with you.

**I am Ross and I am the boss of the Curious Chemical Company.** I will be pulling some strings with my friends in the Government to make sure these spectacles never get produced. You see, I really don't want people seeing what's in the atmosphere because then there might be some difficult questions to answer… questions which I'd rather no one asked.

**I am Eric.** I have just had a visit from a representative of the Government. My spectacles are not to be produced. He said it was in the interests of public safety…

### 💬 Talking and listening

- What would be good and bad about spectacles which could see every gas in the atmosphere?
- Do you think anyone might not want such spectacles to be produced?
- How clean do you think your air is?
- What causes air pollution?
- What do you think the effects of air pollution can be?

# A living atmosphere

Even on a beautifully clear crisp day, our atmosphere is alive with all sorts of things. Fumes from car exhausts, gases from our central heating boilers, smoke from our chimneys, carbon dioxide from our breathing, and methane emissions from places it's best not to mention!

All of these gases and emissions interact in our atmosphere in very complicated ways, which even climate scientists haven't completely figured out yet. Some can be good and bad – even both at the same time. For example, ozone is vital in our upper atmosphere to protect us from the Sun's rays, but lower in the atmosphere it is very dangerous for life. Carbon dioxide helps keep our atmosphere warm – without it, life on Earth may never have developed – but it can also warm our atmosphere up too much, leading to what's known as the 'greenhouse effect'. This greenhouse effect could have very serious consequences for all life on Earth as it changes our climate in ways we can't predict – things like sea-level rises, the melting of the ice caps and more extreme weather patterns.

So what's in our atmosphere is vital for our life, but could also be deadly for us too if its balance is upset. Many scientists believe that our atmosphere is already showing signs of becoming imbalanced – and they think that much of this is because of human activities. They say that if we don't

start being more careful about the stuff we emit into the atmosphere then we may have to pay a very high price for it. So maybe next time you're in a car being driven to school – when you could easily walk – remember that your car's exhaust fumes are harming our atmosphere… and you may have to pay the price for that.

## Active Learning

1. Copy and complete the following table by re-arranging the sources of greenhouse gases so they're beside the correct gas. (Remember: one source could contribute to more than one greenhouse gas.) You can find information about this at www.epa.gov/climatechange/kids/basics/index.html

| Greenhouse gas | Sources |
|---|---|
| Water vapour | Fertilisers for crops |
| Carbon dioxide | Some ordinary kitchen fridges |
| Methane | Evaporation of water |
| Nitrous oxide | Burning fossil fuels |
| Ozone | Some chemical processes |
| Chlorofluorocarbons/ Perfluorocarbons | Agricultural processes such as grazing cows |
| Sulphur hexafluoride | Car exhaust emissions |

2. Draw your own diagram of how the greenhouse effect works and explain how the greenhouse effect could harm life on Earth. See http://earthguide.ucsd.edu/earthguide/diagrams/greenhouse/

3. Once you have found out what the typical sources of greenhouse gases are, you could think about how your own actions contribute to producing greenhouse gases. What changes could you make in your life to reduce your greenhouse gas emissions? (This is sometimes called reducing your 'carbon footprint'.) You can calculate your carbon footprint at http://footprint.wwf.org.uk/

4. Produce a poster which warns people about the possible effects of polluting our atmosphere. You should make it clear what people can do… and what might happen if they don't.

## Progress Check

1. Answer the following:
   a. Name three greenhouse gases.
   b. Explain how two of these gases can be produced.
   c. What harm might a greenhouse effect cause to life on Earth?
   d. What is air pollution and what are the sources of air pollution?
   e. What things do you do which might cause air pollution?
   f. How could you reduce your environmental impact?

2. Discuss this statement: 'Polluting the atmosphere is mostly caused by human activities.'

3. Use the letters of the phrase 'greenhouse effect' to create an acrostic about the issues involved.

### On your own

1. Choose four or five people you know and explain to them how human activity might cause the greenhouse effect. Now tell them about some of the things they could do to reduce their carbon footprint. Get each one to state one thing they will change to reduce their greenhouse gas emissions.

2. The eco-congregation in Scotland has asked churches to reduce their greenhouse gas emissions. Find out about this and about why Christians think looking after our atmosphere is important. See www.ecocongregation.org/scotland/

*It is the annual awards ceremony at the Scottish Fund for Urban Environmentalism. The final award is about to be announced: for the person who has lived the most sustainable life in the past year while living in a city…*

'Ladies and gentlemen, this year's award for the most environmentally sustainable lifestyle goes to… Wayne Albright!' *[applause]*

'Wayne has demonstrated the highest possible levels of sustainable living during the last year, while living on the fourteenth floor of a tower block in Dundee. Wayne produces all his own energy through solar panels and a mini wind turbine on his balcony. Wayne has a room in his flat where he grows most of his food in pots. And what he can't grow himself, he buys from a farm in Carnoustie – taking regular trips there on his bike – or finds growing wild in the nearby countryside. His jaggy nettle soup is said to be the best soup in Dundee. He did ask the council if he could keep some chickens in his flat, but they were having none of that. Another example of environmental short-sightedness with the powers that be I'm afraid… *[agreement from audience]*

Wayne also makes his own clothes, using materials he finds at the local recycling centre. He's there at least once a week and finds it astounding what people throw out. His entire home was furnished using things other people had obviously tired of – most of which was in perfectly good condition. He says he really doesn't understand people's need to replace perfectly good stuff with other things which they'll also throw out in a few months. Wayne only puts a bag of rubbish out for collection by the council every couple of months, finding a use for almost everything.

Interestingly, Wayne is also an RME teacher at the local secondary school, where the pupils have got quite used to his occasionally unusual appearance… Although they can't understand how anyone can possibly live without a mobile phone. Recently, Wayne received a letter from the Scottish Government asking for advice on how to encourage others to live more sustainable lifestyles… Let's hope they listen to him!

Ladies and gentlemen, environmentalist of the year… Wayne Albright.' *[applause]*

## Talking and listening

- How environmentally friendly (sustainable) is your lifestyle?
- How much energy do you think you use in a typical day?
- How do you usually travel?
- Do you recycle? How much? What things?
- How do you think you could live a more environmentally friendly life?

## A sustainable lifestyle

Sustainability means using what we have now in ways which will protect it for the use of future generations. This could be our use of energy or natural resources, our foodstuffs, or any way in which we interact with the natural world. Many people are beginning to realise that we need to think carefully about how we treat nature so that we can obtain what we need without exhausting nature completely.

Most modern lifestyles are pretty hard on the environment. We use incredible amounts of energy for the increasing number of electronic gadgets we have – and a great deal of this energy still comes from things like fossil fuels, which are not really sustainable. We make even the shortest journey by car, and the skies are filled with aircraft going this way and that – again using fuels which have serious environmental consequences, both in getting hold of them and then in their use. We're having to feed increasing populations and so grow more food, and more quickly, which doesn't give the land time to recover and needs chemicals galore to keep going.

And then there's our waste – plastics take thousands of years to decompose, and there are also metals and chemicals which find their way onto our land, into our rivers and seas. Some people are only just waking up to the need to reduce, reuse and recycle. Some are beginning to ask how we can produce more sustainable energy through the power of the wind and the Sun. Some are beginning to question the overuse of the car. Some are beginning to reduce their consumption of all sorts of things. Some are beginning to question if we can go on the way we are without causing harm to nature and ourselves… Can we?

## Active Learning

1. Are you living a sustainable lifestyle? Investigate your own activities and try to answer these questions:
   a. How much do you recycle? Could you do more?
   b. Do you take any journeys by car that could be made in some other way?
   c. How much energy do you use at home? Do you always switch things off when you're not using them?
   d. Where does your food come from? How much do you waste?
   e. What do you do with stuff you no longer want?

2. In your class, compare everyone's answers to the activity above and decide who in your class would win the award for the most environmentally friendly lifestyle. You could make an award and even make it a monthly event.

3. Prepare a mini-project on one aspect of sustainable living from the following choices:
   a. renewable energy
   b. sustainable food production
   c. the environmental benefits of vegetarianism/veganism
   d. reducing, reusing and recycling.

4. In many world religions, sustainable living is closely linked to the concept of 'stewardship'. Find out what this idea means and what it should mean in practice for religious people. You could look at the following websites for ideas:

■ www.christian-ecology.org.uk
■ http://ifees.org.uk/index.php?option=com_content&task=view&id=44&Itemid=58
■ http://urj.org/green/judaism/

 **Progress Check**

1. Answer these questions:
   a. In what ways is Wayne's energy production environmentally friendly?
   b. What evidence is there that Wayne reduces, reuses and recycles?
   c. How does Wayne travel about and why is this environmentally friendly?
   d. What does 'sustainable living' mean?
   e. Do most people in your class live sustainable lifestyles?
   f. In what ways are humans putting pressure on the natural world?

2. Draw up a list of five things your school could do to become a more sustainable place. Perhaps you could present this list to your head teacher and ask him/her to act on it.

3. Make up your own award for an environmentally friendly lifestyle and write out exactly what the award would be given for.

 **On your own**

1. Type 'How to live sustainably' into an Internet search engine and browse through the results. Choose one website and make a short report on what it says for your class.

2. For one week, try to live as sustainable a life as you can. Keep a diary about what you do and how it works out.

# Exploring Islam

5

For me, the simple story of the prophet Muhammad convinces me that he was indeed chosen by God as his messenger. For when you think carefully about the story, the position of Islam in the world today seems all the more incredible and, for me, clear evidence that God is behind it all. Think about it and you'll see what I mean.

Muhammad's young life was not an easy one. He was orphaned at a very young age and then lived with one uncle after another until eventually, in adulthood, he worked in the great city of Mecca as a merchant and also a shepherd. He was in every respect an ordinary person living an ordinary life, until something extraordinary happened…

He seemed to find life in Mecca quite unpleasant in many ways, and he would take to the hills and quietly meditate in caves.

Then one day he returned from a cave with what must have been quite a story, told only to his wife and those closest to him. He said that he had been visited by the angel Jibra'il who had a message from the one, true God. Muhammad was to be God's very last prophet – in a line of prophets throughout the ages – and he was to pass on God's direct words to everyone in the form of the Holy Koran. Yes, Muhammad was to stand up against the mighty people of Mecca to tell them to destroy their wooden and stone idols and to follow one God only.

At first, the powerful people probably ridiculed him – 'what claims he was making!', they must have thought, 'how dare he challenge our power!' Muhammad left the city and went to Madinah, but returned to Mecca many years later. And finally the city was turned from its idol-worshipping ways to the worship of one God alone.

Now, in probably every country of the world you will find Muslims like me. And Islam is one of the largest religions on our planet, yet it all began with just one man and a story which must have sounded quite incredible. For me, had Muhammad been anything other than chosen by God, his story would soon have been forgotten, but it hasn't…

# The prophet Muhammad and Islam

In Islam, the prophet Muhammad is the founder of the faith – he was not any kind of God, just an ordinary man living an ordinary life. Muslims believe that he was chosen by God to pass God's direct words on to humankind. Both Muhammad and the Koran are highly respected in Islam because of their central place in the religion.

Muslims believe that the Koran contains the actual words of God to his people. And that these are his last words, so the Koran is everyone's last chance to get their relationship with God right. Muslims believe that Muhammad is to be respected as the final prophet of God – the last prophet God will send in a line of prophets which included Moses, Abraham and Jesus. In the world today, many countries base their laws and customs on the principles of Islam. Even in countries which are not officially Muslim, there is often a strong Muslim presence.

In today's world there often seems to be a tension between 'the West' and 'the Muslim world', and on both 'sides' it is probably true that some are too quick to judge what they think they see, rather than what is there to be seen. Muslims believe that Islam is a religion of peace, equality, tolerance and concern for others, among many other things. They believe that Islam is a force for good in the world and, like all religion, can make the world a better place.

## Active Learning

1. On a series of world maps, plot the spread of Islam from its beginnings in Mecca and Madinah to its existence today. You could show where Islam is found in the world today and how many people follow this faith.

2. Choose two countries where Islam is the main religion and create a factsheet about the differences in how Islam is expressed in these two countries.

3. In Islam, a central set of beliefs is called the 'five pillars'. Make your own poster about this showing how following most of the five pillars could be done by someone whether they are Muslim or not.

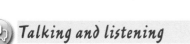

## Talking and listening

- How often do you hear about Islam and Muslims in the world today? Is what you hear positive or negative?
- How do you think those close to Muhammad in his life would have reacted to this story about the visit of the angel in the cave?
- Does the existence of Islam in the world today prove that what happened to Muhammad is true?
- How might you have responded to Muhammad's story?
- Do you think religion helps people to make sense of their lives? How might it do so?

4. There is a strong Muslim community in Scotland. What evidence is there for this where you live (or elsewhere in the country)? You could prepare a PowerPoint presentation of your findings.

### Progress Check

## On your own

1. Visit www.bbc.co.uk/ religion/religions/islam/ and write a report about things you learn about Islam there.

2. If you were able to interview a Muslim about his/her beliefs, what would you ask? If you can actually do so then this would be good. Alternatively, you may be able to find answers to some of your questions on the Internet.

1. Answer these questions based on what you have learned in this chapter:
   a. What do Muslims believe happened to Muhammad in the cave?
   b. Why would a Muslim say that the story of Muhammad is good evidence for the existence of God?
   c. What was Muhammad given in the cave and what do Muslims believe this is?
   d. In which countries of the world will you find Islam today?
   e. What different 'kinds' of Islam are there in the world today? (See chapter 24 on Muslim sects.)

2. Discuss this statement: 'Unfortunately, the media in the West does not always present Islam in a very positive way.'

3. In 60 seconds write down as many things as you can remember about the story of Muhammad.

Now, I could write a book for you about every single one of my beliefs as a Muslim. Many of them would be far too complicated for me to explain, because I don't always understand them myself, and many of them might even be disagreed with by other Muslims. Just like any religion, we have our disagreements within our faith – but differences of opinion are quite normal… quite human. God gave us each a brain so we could think things through for ourselves and not just follow what others tell us to believe. That's what I think anyway.

So I have tried to put together a list of the things I believe. I think most other Muslims would agree with my list, but you'd have to ask them. It's not perfect, but it'll give you the idea:

1.  There is only one God. He is unique, and he chose Muhammad to be his last messenger and to pass on his message.

2.  God's word exists in the Holy Koran. This is God's final word to humanity and is the basis for everything we believe and do in life.

3.  God made the Universe and everything in it. Because of this we have a responsibility to look after everything around us.

4.  A Muslim should submit to the will of God and put what God wants before what he or she wants individually.

5.  A Muslim can express his or her submission to God through prayer, what we eat, how we dress, and how we behave towards others.

6.  Muslims have a special responsibility to care for those in need – no matter what has caused their need and no matter whether they are Muslim or not.

7.  All Islam is one brotherhood (women too) which we call Ummah. This reflects our shared approach to life and gives us rights as well as responsibilities.

8.  At the end of my life, I will have to answer to God for the kind of life that I have lived.

By the way, my faith isn't some kind of hobby that I do in my spare time – it's part of who I am and what makes me me. It gives my life a sense of purpose and meaning too. I don't always understand everything in my faith, but it is like a journey – a personal search which helps me to choose what direction I go in life. How do you decide where your life is going?

### Talking and listening

- How do you decide the direction your life is going in?
- What gives your life meaning and purpose?
- In what ways do you think life is like a journey?
- What would the world be like if everyone put the needs of others before their own?
- This Muslim says he doesn't always understand everything in his faith. Does that matter?

## Contemporary Muslim belief

Like any religion, Islam exists in a changing world that is full of challenges and difficulties. Muslims, like everyone else, have to cope with what life throws at them. In our modern stressful world, this can sometimes be very difficult. Also, like many religions, Islam faces the challenge of bringing its young people up in the faith in a world where there are many distractions and many ways in which a young person can be tempted to go against the teachings of Islam.

Also, like any religion, as Islam moved around the world it has faced the challenge of being true to its own beliefs while adapting to the cultures and countries it has found itself in. For example, Muslims believe that you should obey the laws of the country in which you live, but peacefully speak out against them if they go against the teachings of your faith. This is something which almost all religious people do – no matter which religion they follow.

Muslims also believe that you should be kind and honest and fair and help others. Again, beliefs that they would share with pretty much every other religious person in the world (and most non-religious people too!). Many Muslims are keen to protect their own identity, because they think it is something of value and beneficial to the world. This too is a typical human thing to do and is shared by religious and non-religious people everywhere. Muslims believe that God expects them to follow a certain lifestyle and to make the world a better place… the kind of place God would like it to be.

### Active Learning

1. Have a look at this Muslim's list of Muslim beliefs. Do you think any of them might be disagreed with by other Muslims? Are there any which you could agree with, even if you're not a Muslim?

2. Look through some newspapers or do an Internet search of some news about modern Islam. Read the stories and compare them with the list of Muslim beliefs you have read in this section. Do any of the news stories get Islam wrong?

3. In some countries of the world, Muslims say that they have experienced 'Islamophobia'. This is a form of discrimination against people because they are Muslim. Discuss why people sometimes discriminate against others. Why do you think Islam has experienced this, perhaps more than any other religion in the modern world?

4. In some countries in 'the West', many expressions of Islam have been challenged by people – including governments – such as the wearing of the burkah in France. Is it ever right to stop people expressing their religious beliefs?

1. Answer these questions:
   a. In your own words, write down three things Muslims believe.
   b. Do you think that any of the Muslim beliefs you have learned about are considered more important than others?
   c. In what ways is Islam presented negatively in the modern world and why is this?
   d. How do you think following Islam helps a Muslim make sense of life?
   e. What pressures are young Muslims under in the modern world?
   f. Should people be able to express their beliefs however they want?

2. Discuss this statement: 'To live at peace with our neighbours, we first have to understand them.' What do you think this statement means and do you agree with it?

3. In your own words, write out what you think are the three most important beliefs in Islam.

 **On your own**

1. Find out what the five pillars of Islam are all about and how they help Muslims to make sense of their lives.

2. Have a look at the website of a Muslim charity and report on how they put their beliefs about helping others into action. (For example, see www.muslimaid.org/)

*Billy is interviewing his friend, who he calls his Muslim pal Kamal…*

**Billy:** Right Kamal, see that stuff we learned in RME, you don't really pray five times a day do you?

**Kamal:** Well I do try… but sometimes it's more difficult than others. Like early in the morning. I'm a teenager. I need my sleep… it's a scientific fact.

**Billy:** So does Allah like, punish you for that?

**Kamal:** No, I'm sure Allah understands. And anyway, if I missed one prayer time I usually try to catch up as soon as I can.

**Billy:** Is it true that you just stop what you're doing and pray wherever you are when it's prayer time?

**Kamal:** Sort of… Well, if I was a surgeon or something doing brain surgery I'd not be likely to say 'Hey, can you just hold this scalpel for a minute while I nip off and pray.' You try to stick to the times, but if you can't that's okay.

**Billy:** So what's with all the bowing and kneeling and stuff?

**Kamal:** Well that's the Salat prayers and we use our body to express what's going on inside. Like you at the football – you're not likely to stand still there are you? Our body outwardly expresses our submission to the will of Allah. It also shows that I'm a Muslim and we should be proud of that.

**Billy:** And do you need to do it five times a day?

**Kamal:** We look at it as a way of showing who we are, and a way to remember Allah. If we can make time for him when we're really busy in the middle of the day, or when we're really knackered late at night, then that shows how important Allah is for us.

**Billy:** I've seen you pray, it looks like you just say the same thing over and over again – isn't that a bit pointless?

**Kamal:** Not really. In the Salat prayers we're mostly reciting bits of the Koran and following a kind of formula, but there's Dua prayers too.

**Billy:** Do what?

**Kamal:** Dua prayers. These are prayers about anything that matters to you. Say maybe if someone is sick or something, you ask Allah to watch over them.

**Billy:** And does Allah always answer?

**Kamal:** Aw come on Billy, you know better than that. We believe that Allah knows what's best. You'll hear Muslims say 'Insh' Allah' all the time, which means 'God-willing'. If Allah wants it to happen it'll happen.

**Billy:** But you pray anyway?

**Kamal:** Yeah. There's no reason why we can't ask Allah – can't hurt.

**Billy:** See at our age, do you not feel a bit weird praying, cos' most people our age aren't exactly dead holy?

**Kamal:** No, I don't feel weird. It's just part of who I am as a person. Praying gives my day a kind of rhythm, which I like… And it makes me feel part of something much bigger. It helps me to make sense of things – even when the world sometimes seems pretty crazy.

**Billy:** You actually make it sound pretty reasonable.

**Kamal:** You could give it a try.

**Billy:** But I'm not a Muslim.

**Kamal:** I'm sure Allah would listen to you anyway…

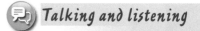

### Talking and listening

- Have you ever prayed?
- What do you know about the positions Muslims take up when praying?
- If God knows everything, is there any need to tell him things?
- What kinds of things might a Muslim offer Dua prayers for?
- How important is it to take time during your daily life to think about what life is all about?

# Prayer in Islam

Many people have seen the ritual set of prayers which Muslims are expected to carry out five times a day. There are even timetables produced so that all Muslims everywhere can be praying at the same time – no matter where in the world they live. The physical act of prayer shows that a Muslim is submitting to the will of Allah.

But prayer is more than that. Prayer helps Muslims to express their identity – to show who they are. For example, in the Salat prayers Muslims stand side by side showing that all are equal in the eyes of Allah. It's also a way to live out your relationship with God as you give up the things you would be doing at the set prayer times.

Prayer in Islam is like prayer in many other religions – a very personal thing where you thank God for what you have and ask him to provide for others too, especially those in need. Even though you pray, you don't expect God to provide everything you ask for. You trust that he'll make the right decision in the circumstances. Muslims, like other religious people, believe that God is much wiser than humans and will do the right thing – but it doesn't hurt to ask. For Muslims, prayer helps to make sense of life by bringing something holy into the ordinary world.

## Active Learning

1. The Salat prayers involve a series of body positions – do your own sketches of these and describe what's said and what the position indicates. You can find information about this at www.bbc.co.uk/religion/galleries/salah/

2. What kinds of things might a Muslim pray for in the Dua prayers? Discuss this in class and come up with a top ten. These could be personal, local or international. The website http://duas.org/ will also give you some ideas.

3. The timetable for Salat prayers is followed by Muslims so that everyone prays together. Find the most recent timetable (try www.salahtimes.com/Web/Pages/ViewPrayerTimesForMonthYear.aspx?PlaceID=25799). Which prayer times would be difficult for you this week? How might this timetable affect your life if you had to follow it (or does affect it if you do, of course)?

4. Prayer doesn't have to be words or body positions, it can also be your actions. What things might Muslims also do in their daily life to worship God? (Look back to your work on the five pillars to help you.)

 ## On your own

1. Find a magazine or newspaper article which you think a Muslim (or anyone) might want to pray about. Write the prayer you think could be said.

2. Choose one other religion you have looked at in RME. In what ways is Muslim prayer similar or different to this religion's prayers?

 **Progress Check**

1. Answer these questions:
   a. How many times are Muslims supposed to pray every day?
   b. What names are given to these prayer times?
   c. What would a Muslim do if he or she missed a prayer time?
   d. What's the difference between Salat and Dua prayer?
   e. Why might some of the prayer times be more difficult than others?
   f. Why do Muslims pray? (You can suggest as many reasons as you like.)

2. Discuss this: 'If God knows everything, why does anyone need to pray?'

3. Write out your own set of prayer instructions for someone who has recently become a Muslim.

'Ashhadu Alla Ilaha Illa Allah Wa Ashhadu Anna Muhammad Rasulu Allah'

'There is no God but Allah and Muhammad is the prophet of Allah'

I am a Sunni Muslim. Most other Muslims in the world are Sunni like me. We believe that there is no God but Allah and Muhammad is his prophet. We follow the five pillars of Islam, and we pray, fast, celebrate life and treat others according to the teachings of Islam. These are found in the Koran, which is the holy word of Allah, and in the Hadith, which are the sayings and actions of the prophet (peace and blessings be upon him). I believe that Allah made the Universe and all that is in it is his. I believe that a Muslim must submit to the will of Allah and that we will each be judged by Allah for the way in which we have lived our lives. I believe we should protect the weak and help those who need our help.

'Ashhadu Alla Ilaha Illa Allah Wa Ashhadu Anna Muhammad Rasulu Allah Ali-yyun wali-yyu-llāh'

'There is no God but Allah and Muhammad is the prophet of Allah. Ali is the friend of Allah'

I am a Shia Muslim. In Islam about ten per cent of Muslims are Shia Muslims like me. We believe that there is no God but Allah and Muhammad is his prophet. We follow the five pillars of Islam, and we pray, fast, celebrate life and treat others according to the teachings of Islam. These are found in the Koran, which is the holy word of Allah, and in the Hadith, which are the sayings and actions of the prophet (peace and blessings be upon him). I believe that Allah made the Universe and all that is in it is his. I believe that a Muslim must submit to the will of Allah and that we will each be judged by Allah for the way in which we have lived our lives. I believe we should protect the weak and help those who need our help.

### 💬 Talking and listening

- What differences can you see between the two types of Muslim here?
- After saying Muhammad's name, Muslims will say 'Peace be upon him'. Why do you think this is said?
- Why do you think religions usually have different groups within them?
- When a religion splits into more than one group, do you think this is a good thing or not?
- What kinds of things do people in the world today disagree about?

# Sunnis and Shi'ites

When Muhammad died, his followers were not sure who should take up his position as leader of the faith. One group, the Sunni, thought that the successor (or Caliph) to Muhammad would be the person best suited to the job, and the person Muhammad's followers agreed should get the position. They therefore chose Abu Bakr – a friend of Muhammad – as his successor. The Shi'ites, however, thought that Muhammad's successor should be one of his own family. They thought that Ali, Muhammad's brother-in-law, should be his successor. Abu Bakr was chosen as leader, but the disagreement continued.

As time went on, the split between the followers of Abu Bakr and Ali grew wider and each group started to choose their own leaders. The split remains to this day. Sunni and Shia Muslims began to treat one set of Hadith (the sayings and actions of Muhammad) as more important than others and so some differences in beliefs and values developed. Also, as Sunnis and Shi'ites drifted apart into different countries, they started to change their practices in some ways too. So what started off as a disagreement about a leader became two separate groups within the one religion of Islam.

## Active Learning

1. Find out how many Sunni and Shia Muslims there are in the world today and mark their presence of a world map. Which countries are mainly Shia and which are mainly Sunni? (See http://en.wikipedia.org/wiki/List_of_countries_by_Muslim_population)

2. Find a timeline of Sunni and Shia Caliphs and make your own poster about this. (See www.bbc.co.uk/religion/religions/islam/subdivisions/sunnishia_1.shtml)

3. There are other groups within Islam too, such as the Sufis and the Ismailis. Find out what other groups of Muslims there are in the world and the ways in which they differ from most Sunni and Shia Muslims. Display your findings.

4. Look at any other religions you have studied in RME. Do they have groups within them too? Discuss the reasons why you think people often split into smaller groups after they have begun as one. You could look at this under the headings:
   - changes in belief
   - changes in values
   - changes in practices and traditions
   - geographical spread
   - important historical events
   - different ways of understanding the faith.

**Progress Check**

1. Answer these questions:
   a. What is a Sunni Muslim?
   b. What is a Shia Muslim?
   c. Roughly what percentage of the world's Muslims are Sunnis or Shi'ites?
   d. Why did Sunnis and Shi'ites split up in the first place?
   e. Where are most Sunnis and Shi'ites in the world today?
   f. In what way is the Sunni and Shi'ite Shahadah (the statement of faith on page 75) different?

2. Discuss this: 'Differences of opinion in a religion make it stronger not weaker.'

3. Write the words Sunni and Shia on a piece of paper in different colours. Now pass this round in class and get people to write one piece of information on the sheet each. The thing they write should match the colour of the word Sunni or Shia depending upon which group it relates to.

 *On your own*

1. There have been tensions between Iran and Iraq in recent years and some say that the tensions have been made worse by Sunni and Shia differences. Is this true? Do your own research on the Internet on this issue.

2. Choose one Muslim country and find out what percentage of its population is Sunni and Shia. You may even find that cities in this country have different areas within the city which are mostly Shia or Sunni. Report your findings.

### Talking and listening

- In what kind of building do you think this art can be found?
- Why do you think so much effort has been put into this art?
- Do you think this art will help people in their religious life or be distracting?
- What kinds of things are not shown in this art?
- Why do you think religious people create art?

# Features of Islamic art

Just like in any culture of the world, you will find art in the faith of Islam. It might be in holy buildings such as mosques, or it might be in ordinary buildings. It could be on the cover of a Koran or simply hanging in someone's home. It could also just as well be a pot as a great painting.

Islamic art has a feature which is a little unusual: it does not include any images of people or animals. Most art in Islam is either made out of Arabic words (known as calligraphy) or is made out of geometric patterns. Islamic art isn't really concerned with portraying the physical side of life – such as landscapes and objects – it is more concerned with trying to express something spiritual about the world and everything in it. Much of the art in Islam is about things to do with the faith of Islam, but it can also convey very ordinary things too.

The reason that Islamic art avoids showing living things is because it is thought that having images of living things might lead to 'idolatry' – worshipping things rather than Allah. When Muhammad turned the city of Mecca to Islam, one of the first things to be done was throwing out the statues and images in the Ka'aba. Islamic art, like all art, tries to help people to understand the world in which we live… it just does so a little differently.

## Active Learning

1. Islamic art covers all sorts of artforms – from pottery to ceramic tiles to painting and so on. Create your own display of Muslim art in your school using images from the Internet and write a piece of information about each thing on display. You could also add Post-Its for people to write up what the art 'says' to them.

2. In a typical mosque you will usually find many examples of Islamic art. Make a list of the kinds of things you might find. Use the Internet to find pictures of the inside and outside of mosques, or you can visit a virtual mosque at www.thebcom.org/mosquetour/index.htm

3. Create your own piece of Muslim art. It could be calligraphy, geometric mosaics or a painting, etc.

4. Islamic art may use images of important sites in Islam. Find out which sites and buildings might be likely to be used and create a presentation using images of these sites. Are there any differences here between Sunni and Shia sites?

 **On your own**

1. In Islam, music may also be part of religious life. Find out about the music of the Sufis and about the singing of the call to prayer. Why do you think Muslims do not sing as part of their worship?

2. Islamic architecture is also a form of art – and is generally very specific to the Arab world. Find two or three examples of Islamic architecture and explain how this is different from 'Western' architecture.

**Progress Check**

1. Answer these questions:
   a. What is the main difference between Islamic art and any other kind of art?
   b. What kinds of things might Islamic art be other than paintings?
   c. What is calligraphy?
   d. How is geometry used in Islamic art?
   e. Is all Islamic art about religion?
   f. Why are images of living things not permitted in Islam?

2. Discuss or debate this statement: 'Creating art for a mosque is an expensive waste of time.'

3. Write out three rules for a Muslim artist.

# Science and religion

# 6

As a scientist, what I think is probably happening is that somehow the temporal lobes of the brain are being stimulated – 'switched on' if you like. These are at the side of the brain and we think that they're a rather complicated area where what we see and experience is made sense of by the brain.

What's probably happening is that these lobes are switched on by some outside stimulus. For example, some kind of chemical might be doing it. This could be in an ordinary medicine or it could be in a drug taken for some other reason. The brain's chemistry gets altered and it thinks it sees what isn't there.

It could also be something to do with oxygen supply to the brain. We know that when people don't get all the oxygen they need they can often see and experience very odd things indeed.

There's also the possibility that illness and stress can affect the brain – and the brain tries to cope with these things by producing pleasant experiences to make you feel better.

Of course, many of the people who have these experiences want to have them, and may get themselves whipped up into a state where they see and experience exactly what they want to. They could do this by singing, dancing, chanting – there's lots of ways.

There's electricity too. Your brain is full of electric currents – if these get affected by electricity from somewhere else then who knows what you might think you see, hear or feel. Also, perhaps the people who have these things are just mistaken – fooled by optical illusions.

And last but not least, perhaps these people are just telling lies in the hope of getting some attention…

*As a Christian, I think everything the scientist has described is simply wrong. God does make himself known to people. Why is that so hard to accept?*

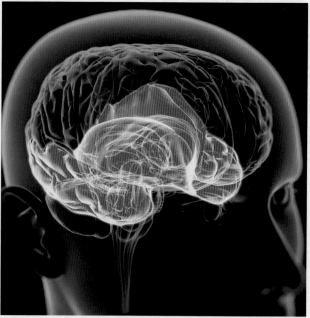

## Talking and listening

- What do you think a religious experience is?
- Do you think when people see something like a God or important religious figure that they are really seeing it?
- Why might people make mistakes about this kind of thing?
- Would people tell lies about this? If so, why?
- Have you ever had an experience which you can't explain reasonably?

# Explaining religious experiences

This can be anything from seeing God or some other religious figure to getting an answer to a prayer, to having a feeling that there's something out there bigger than you are. Many people who have had religious experiences find that the experience changes their life – almost always for the better. Many people feel that religious experiences are solid proof that their religion is true. For many religious people, having a religious experience is quite normal and only to be expected when you believe in supernatural beings such as God.

People all over the world have had what they believe are religious experiences throughout history – no matter which religion they follow. However, many religious people have never had any kind of religious experience, even people who would really like to have one! Scientific investigation about religious experiences has come up with some of the alternative suggestions which the scientist on the previous page explained. For many scientists, there is almost always a more reasonable explanation for what people think is a religious experience (though of course many scientists are religious too!).

However, for religious people, having these experiences is just part of what it means to be religious and proves to them that their faith is real. What do you think?

## Active Learning

1. The following may be features of a religious experience. For each one, discuss what you think the person might actually experience and any possible alternative explanations for what is happening:
   a. Seeing God or some religious figure (Mary, Krishna, etc.).
   b. Hearing the voice of a religious figure, though not seeing them.
   c. Feeling the presence of God or a religious figure.
   d. Feeling 'guided' to do something.
   e. Feeling a sense of being part of something bigger in the Universe.
   f. Experiencing a miracle.

2. Find out about one or more of the following. Explain what happened to them and how their life changed after this experience:
   a. Teresa of Avila
   b. Charles Wesley
   c. Cameron Mackenzie
   d. Nicky Cruz
   e. Saint Paul (Saul of Tarsus).

3. Many claim that some religious activities are designed to get your brain 'worked up' into a state where a religious experience is likely. What do you think about this? Find some examples of religious worship which might do this and discuss what's happening. You could look, for example, at Charismatic Christian worship or repetitive meditation in Buddhism or the swirling of the Sufis and so on.

4. Someone tells you that they saw God standing at the bottom of their bed one night and that God has asked them to pass a message on to the world. What questions would you ask this person about their experience? How would you investigate their experience?

**On your own**

1. For many people the 'near-death experience' counts as a religious experience. Find out what this is, and what different views there are about it.

2. Write your own conversation between two people, one of whom believes that religious experiences are proof of the existence of God and one who doesn't.

1. Answer the following questions:
   a. What is meant by a religious experience?
   b. Describe two types of religious experience.
   c. Describe two alternative explanations for religious experiences.
   d. Describe the religious experience of one person you have studied.
   e. What questions would you ask this person about their experience if you could?
   f. Do you think religious experiences prove that religion is true?

2. Discuss this statement: 'There is always a perfectly reasonable explanation for a religious experience.'

3. Make up an acrostic about 'religious experience' which uses all the letters of the phrase (such as '**r**eally **e**xtraordinary **l**ightning **i**n **G**od's...').

*Humans behave badly because they have separated themselves from God. They have tried to make themselves God but, because they could never do this, they sometimes end up behaving towards each other – and the world they live in – in terrible ways. The first man, Adam, rejected God by disobeying God's commands and so fell from God's grace. We call this the Fall, and think that this is how sin came into the world… and has been with us ever since.*

*Every bad action (or sin) a human carries out is a matter of personal choice. They cannot blame anyone else for it – it is the responsibility of each one of us to do what is right. Now some of my fellow Christians think that the Devil has a role to play in turning people away from God and towards evil actions. I think the Devil exists, but I think we can resist his temptations if we want to. Humans need to turn to God – then evil and suffering will end.*

Humans behave badly for many complicated reasons. Doing bad things is a mixture of nature and nurture. Nature is what we're born with – our genetic inheritance in our DNA, which makes some people calm and others aggressive. There's not too much you can do to control your inheritance. Perhaps in the future we'll be able to genetically engineer the badness out of people and that will be an end to murders and wars and so on. But then again, perhaps not. People who do bad things may do them because of the effects of nurture. This is about how you're brought up – the example your parents and peers set you, and what the society you live in thinks is 'normal'. If you're brought up in a particular way then it can't help affecting the person you are.

Evil and suffering will only ever end if we can put right nature's DNA mistakes **and** if we can live our lives as a good example for others. How can anyone even think of blaming a Devil in the twenty-first century!?!

### 🗨 Talking and listening

- Do you think someone can be 'born bad'?
- Can you blame your upbringing for your bad actions?
- Do you think people do bad things because of the Devil?
- Do you think that evil caused by people will ever end?
- When did you last do something bad? Why did you do it?

1. Imagine that someone called Kellie is in prison for murder. She killed a man on a bus while he was reading his newspaper. There was no reason for the attack and she doesn't even know why she did it – she's not normally violent. What kinds of things would you want to find out about Kellie to work out why she committed this murder? Draw up a plan of investigation about Kellie's crime.

2. Christians believe that the Fall brought human evil (sin) into the world. Find out about this story in the Bible. What happened and why was it the cause of sin? Discuss in your class and think about whether or not this is an explanation for humans behaving badly. Could Kellie blame Adam for her crime?

3. Go through some newspapers and find some stories of things that humans do which seem hard to explain. Now, investigate each story as you did for the example of Kellie above. What questions would you like to ask about this example of bad behaviour?

4. Imagine that a technique (or a drug) was invented by scientists which could stop a person ever doing anything bad. Should that technique or drug be put to use? Discuss this in class and note any interesting answers.

## Explaining human behaviour

So far we've only thought about bad behaviour, but the same could have been written about good behaviour. What makes humans behave the way they do? If only we knew for sure! Most religious people believe that humans must take personal responsibility for their actions. In particular, they must live the kind of lives God wants them to – so that bad things will no longer happen.

Of course, most religious people also accept that your genetic inheritance, and when, where and how you're brought up, have important effects upon your behaviour. The more science investigates human behaviour, the more it becomes clear that our behaviour seems to be a very complex thing – a mixture of nature and nurture.

But… does that excuse us from our actions? Can we blame our DNA? Can we blame our parents and how they brought us up, or the examples set by our friends? Can we blame the circumstances of our lives? Or do we need to take responsibility for our choices or listen to what God is telling us?

1. Discuss and answer the following questions:
   a. What is meant by 'the Fall'?
   b. What do Christians mean by the word 'sin'?
   c. How might the Devil be an explanation for people doing bad things?
   d. What do scientists mean by nature and nurture?
   e. How might nature and/or nurture cause someone to do bad things?
   f. Would all religious people disagree with everything the scientist has said in the introduction?

2. Debate this in class: 'Everyone is personally responsible for their own actions, no matter how bad their upbringing was.'

3. Choose twelve words from the introduction – six from the religious person and six from the scientist. Write these on separate cards and place them face down. Now, against the clock, turn them over and put them in the correct category: 'religious explanation for bad behaviour' or 'scientific explanation for bad behaviour'.

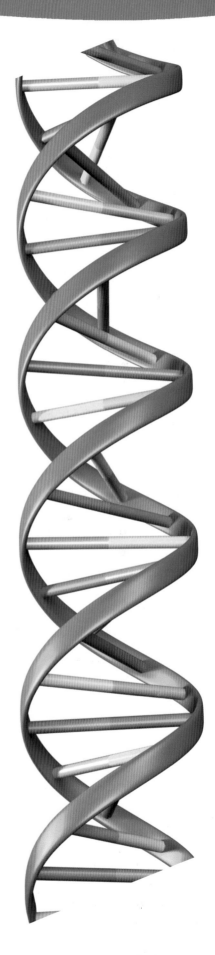

## On your own

1. Find out more about the nature/nurture debate in science and psychology and prepare a presentation on your findings. How much nature and how much nurture do moderns scientists/psychologists think go into causing bad behaviour? The website **www.revisionworld.co.uk/level/psychology/issues-and-debates-psychology/nature-nurture-debate-1** should help.

2. Many argue that criminals should not only be punished, they should be re-educated (because their crimes were the result of nature/nurture influences). Ask a variety of people what they think about this and report your findings to your class.

**Bob:** It's nothing more than a collection of chemicals.

**Rob:** You could think of everyone that way.

**Bob:** It can't feel anything.

**Rob:** How can you be so sure about that?

**Bob:** It doesn't think.

**Rob:** So being a person is only possible if you can think? Does that mean that intelligent people are more of a person than people who aren't very bright?

**Bob:** It's not a person.

**Rob:** But it could be one day, as long as it's left to get on with its life.

**Bob:** Just because something might be something one day doesn't mean it is now.

**Rob:** You've lost me now. When exactly does it start being a person then?

**Bob:** Well, no one's really sure about that.

**Rob:** You're sure enough to end its life.

**Bob:** It's not a life.

**Rob:** How can it not be a life?

**Bob:** Okay, it's a potential life.

**Rob:** Not if you have your way.

**Bob:** Look, the potential benefits of its use far outweigh the problems.

**Rob:** Have you asked it if it agrees with that?

**Bob:** Now you're being silly, it can't communicate what it wants.

**Rob:** So because it can't communicate, you think it's perfectly okay to take advantage of it and destroy it? Should that apply to all living things which can't communicate – like animals or people in a coma?

**Bob:** Come on, it has no self-awareness.

**Rob:** Neither do some people when they are ill or unconscious… or asleep for that matter.

**Bob:** Look, I know it's not ideal, but think of how many people we can help through what we learn by doing this.

**Rob:** So, it's okay to sacrifice one living thing for another, even if that living thing has no say in the matter at all?

**Bob:** Well yes, but I'll say it again: it's not really a living thing in the same way as you and me.

**Rob:** What is it then?

**Bob:** Something else…

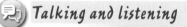

### Talking and listening

- When do you think human life begins?
- Do you have to be able to think to be a human?
- Is it right to destroy something to benefit something else?
- If something can't feel pain, is it okay to hurt it?
- Should all human life be protected from harm?

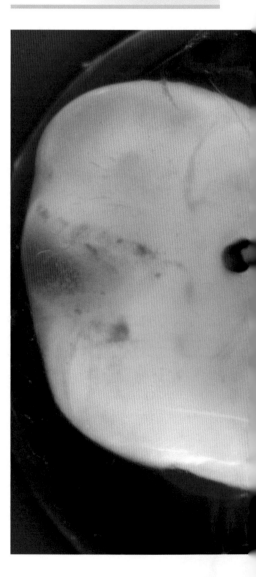

# Using embryos

In Britain, you can use what are known as pre-embryos for scientific research right up to the fourteenth day of their development after fertilisation. After this, it is thought that the embryos might 'feel pain' and so should not be used for research. Any embryo which is not returned to a woman's womb must be destroyed after the fourteenth day.

Some scientists think that using pre-embryos will help us to understand illness and disease and perhaps find cures. Some think that what we learn from research using pre-embryos cannot be learned any other way and so is extremely important. Some people, however, are very concerned about embryo research. They think that it is using a developing human to do experiments which you'd never do on a developed human. Supporters of embryo research argue that pre-embryos are not human in the full sense of the word. But those who disagree with using embryos say that they are potential humans – if left to grow naturally they could become perfectly normal adult human beings.

The whole issue is very complicated and is linked to two important questions:

■ What is a human being?
■ What is acceptable to do to a human being?

Is a pre-embryo human or only partly human? What do you think?

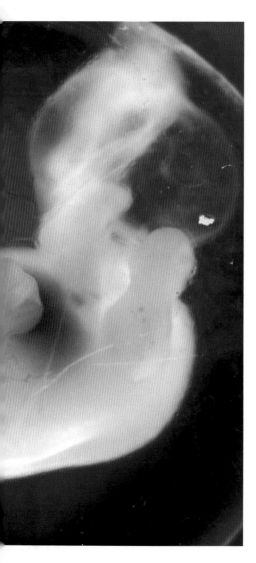

## Active Learning

1. Create your own diagram of the development of a human being from conception to birth. You should describe what is happening at each stage and suggest what stage of 'being human' you think the pre-embryo, embryo and foetus is. A website with this information is at http://en.wikibooks.org/wiki/Human_Physiology/Pregnancy_and_birth

2. What kinds of research are done on pre-embryos and what are the arguments for and against it? Produce your own report on the topic. You could split your report into two sections, outlining the arguments for and against using embryos for research.

3. Many people believe that the argument about the use of embryos is linked to the belief that life is sacred from the moment of conception. Produce your own information sheet about this belief. (See www.christian.org.uk/briefingpapers/embryoexperiments.htm)

4. What makes something human? In groups, discuss this and write up the things that make something human (such as 'ability to think'). You could write the 'more important' things in large letters and the less important things in smaller ones.

1. Answer these questions after your research in this area:
   a. What is a pre-embryo and when does it become an embryo?
   b. What is meant by a 'potential person'?
   c. What is meant by the 'sanctity of life'?
   d. Why might someone think that using an embryo is a 'necessary evil'?
   e. What kinds of research are pre-embryos used for?
   f. In your opinion, is a pre-embryo human?

2. Debate this statement: 'Using embryos for research at any stage of their development is always wrong.'

3. Write as many questions as you can about the use of pre-embryos for research. These questions should cover:
   - the science of embryo research
   - why someone would support embryo research
   - why someone would oppose embryo research.

 *On your own*

1. The Roman Catholic Church is particularly outspoken in its views about embryo research. Find out what its views are by looking on the Internet.

2. Write out your own views on embryo research and explain why you feel this way about the topic.

*Ricky and Nicky are visiting the family planning clinic…*

**Doctor:** So, then, you're trying to start a family are you? Are there any particular difficulties you're facing with that?

**Ricky:** *[laughs]* Oh no Doc, everything's fine in that department.

**Nicky:** Yes, all's well… We just wanted to find out how we make sure our baby is intelligent.

**Doctor:** Get it to a good school for a start, I'd say.

**Ricky:** Well, no Doc, that's not exactly what we mean…

**Nicky:** No, we want to make sure it's really clever *before* it's born.

**Doctor:** There's really no way of checking that I'm afraid. You'll just have to hope for the best.

**Ricky:** We'd rather not. What we really need is a scientist who'll fiddle about with the DNA of our embryo to make sure that it is intelligent when it's born.

**Doctor:** That just isn't possible.

**Ricky:** But we're disgustingly rich and we could make it worth your while – if you know what I mean? All we want is for you to genetically engineer our embryo to make it a little smarter.

**Doctor:** I'm not sure what you've been reading but, first of all, I don't have anything like that kind of expertise. And, even if I could find someone who did, genetically engineering embryos for that kind of thing is completely illegal.

**Nicky:** We can sort out the legal side of things – don't you worry about that. All we need is for you to find us a scientist who'd take the job on.

**Doctor:** But even if I had the slightest idea where to find such a person – and I doubt if that would ever be possible – genetically engineering a human would be so unpredictable and dangerous that you really wouldn't want to risk it.

**Ricky:** We know it's risky… life's risky. But we know what we want, and we *always* get what we want.

**Doctor:** Not in this case. No scientist would take the personal and professional risks.

**Nicky:** We have found, in our experience, that if the price is right, anyone will do anything.

**Doctor:** But it's wrong! You can't play God with this kind of thing…

**Nicky:** Oh but we can… And we'll do a better job of it than God does!

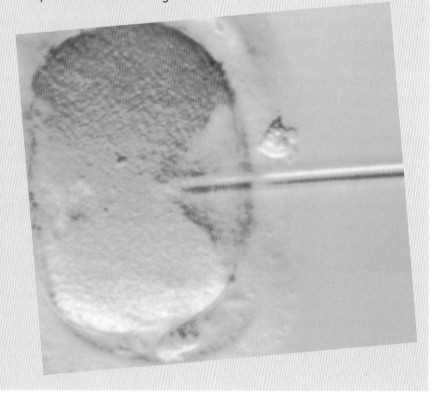

## Talking and listening

- If you could choose the kind of child you have, would you?
- What features in a child do you think most people would choose if they were able to?
- Would meddling with an embryo's genetic information in this way be 'playing God'? (And would there be anything wrong with that?)
- What might the world be like if people could do this kind of thing?
- What kinds of risks might there be with changing the DNA of an embryo?

# Genetic engineering possibilities

Genetic engineering involves altering the DNA of a living thing to make it turn out one way rather than another. It can also include cloning, where DNA from one living thing is replaced by DNA from another. At the moment, genetic engineering is illegal and, besides, science hasn't yet been able to clearly identify which bits of DNA match up with what features – or even if they do. All that is possible at the moment is the screening of embryos for genetic illnesses and then making a decision about whether the embryo should be allowed to grow or not. This is known as therapeutic genetic engineering.

Science fiction is forever throwing up the idea of 'designer babies'. These are children who have been genetically engineered to be clever or super-fit or beautiful and so on. This is known as cosmetic genetic engineering. At the moment, genetically modifying a human embryo for cosmetic purposes is banned everywhere. But who is to say that it will stay that way?

Supporters of genetic engineering say that people should have the choice about the kind of child they have – and if science can help them do that, then why not? Opponents of genetic engineering say that this would be humans meddling about with nature – and could result in all sorts of possible horrors, perhaps even to the development of new diseases which could wipe out human life. They also add that this would be humans 'playing God' and they wonder if humans could handle that ability. Those who think genetic engineering is a good thing say that humans play God every time they give a sick person medicine.

Should we be able to choose what our children become?

## Active Learning

1. Carry out the following survey and display your findings. Ask as many people as you can these questions:
   - If you could have a 'designer baby' and it was totally risk-free, would you?
   - What qualities would you want the child to have?

2. If genetic engineering was not allowed for cosmetic reasons (such as good looks) but was for medical ones (such as wiping out some genetic illnesses), would this be a good thing? Discuss in class and list the pros and cons of genetically changing embryos to rid them of inherited illnesses.

3. What do the world's religions think about genetic engineering of humans? Choose two or three religions you have studied, look on the Internet and write about their views.

4. Some have said that if genetic engineering was ever allowed then only the rich could afford it. The world would then be full of people who were genetically engineered and those who weren't. What problems might this cause? Write a short story about such a world.

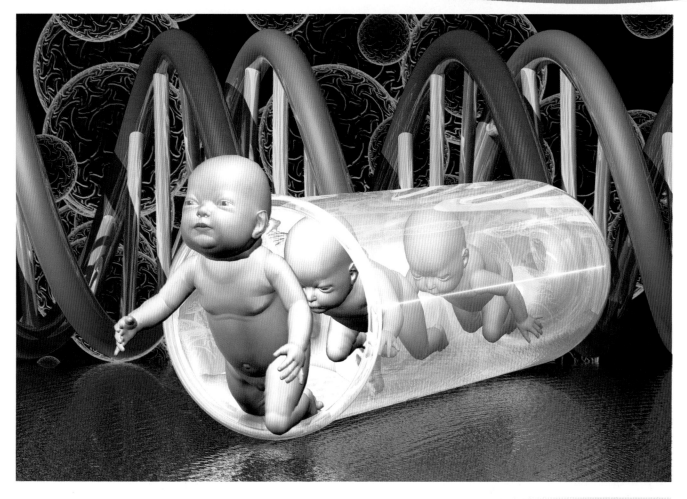

## Progress Check

1. Discuss and answer these questions:
   a. What is meant by 'genetic engineering'?
   b. What's the difference between cosmetic and therapeutic genetic engineering?
   c. What's a designer baby?
   d. Why do you think producing designer babies is currently illegal?
   e. What does the doctor in the introduction say are the problems with genetic engineering?
   f. What do some people mean by saying that genetic engineering is 'playing God'?

2. Debate this in class: 'People should have the right to choose the kind of child they have.'

3. Imagine that the Government has made producing designer babies legal. A protest march is arranged where supporters and opponents of this will march to express their views. Design a placard which you could carry to express your views.

## On your own

1. At the moment, genetically modified (GM) crops are produced perfectly legally. Find out which crops are genetically modified and why, and why some people are against this. (See www.greenpeace. org/international/en/ campaigns/agriculture/)

2. In how many different ways might people 'play God' already? Make up a list of as many things as you can think of. For example, taking a pill for a headache interferes with the natural processes of having a headache.

**Dan:** There comes a point where a person is no longer a person. Maybe they are lying in some hospital bed all wired up with tubes everywhere and nothing going on inside their head. That's not a person any more, it's just a body. For me, the person that used to be inside that body has gone and it's just a physical shell – not a human being in any way that I understand…

**Anne:** No, I don't agree. You have no idea what's going on in that person's head. Just because some machine can't pick up the person's thoughts doesn't mean that he or she isn't having any. Perhaps the person is much more aware than you think – just not able to communicate that to us. Imagine how awful it would be if they could hear and understand us talking about switching their life-support off and do nothing to tell us that they didn't want that to happen.

**Dan:** But if the person can't decide to end their own life, shouldn't we make that decision for them?

**Anne:** Based on what? It's not that simple you know…

**Dan:** Well okay, maybe that's not a nice simple black and white issue. But when someone wants to end their life they should be allowed to do it with the help of science. Some people just get to the stage where they don't want to go on any more. They don't want to suffer and they don't want to become helpless and dependent on others. When they feel their life is no longer worth living, we should let medical staff help them to end it.

**Anne:** No, I don't agree. Should we really put doctors under that kind of pressure? And anyway, who's to say that the person really knows what they're doing? Maybe they're just trying to avoid being a burden to their family. Maybe they're just feeling a bit down. Instead of agreeing to help them kill themselves, we should be supporting them and looking after them. And anyway, who's to decide what kind of a life is worth living and what isn't?

**Dan:** The person whose life it is.

**Anne:** And are they in the best state of mind to make that kind of decision?

### Talking and listening

- When do you think human life ends?
- Does your life belong to you?
- Is someone unconscious and on a life-support machine still alive? Are they still a person?
- Should people have the right to end their life if they want to?
- Should people be able to ask a doctor to help them end their life?

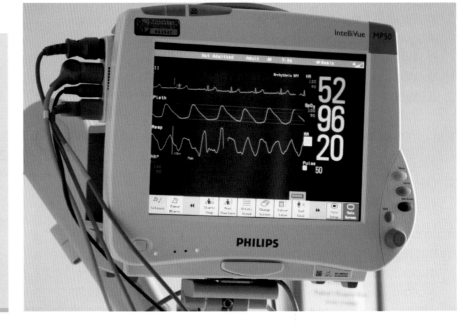

# Voluntary and involuntary euthanasia

Involuntary euthanasia is where a person is thought of as clinically brain-dead (though their heart may be beating and they may still be breathing with the help of a life-support machine). Or perhaps in a persistent vegetative state (PVS) which means there's no 'normal' brain activity going on.

In such situations, some people think that the life-support machine should be switched off and the person allowed to die. Others think that the kindest thing is to give the person some medicine which ends their life – because their life is no longer really a life at all. Some disagree with this because they believe that it is never right to end a person's life. Life, they say, is sacred and so should not be ended artificially, even though they might agree with 'letting a person die'.

Voluntary euthanasia is where a person decides that they no longer want to live and want a doctor to help them kill themselves. Supporters of this say that it's every person's right to choose when and how to die. Some disagree and say that no one has the right to take their own life (or ask someone to help them do so). They may argue that, because life is sacred, the only person who has the right to end it is God.

It's more complex than that though... Some religious people agree that there comes a point where life is no longer life and so helping a person to die is the kindest thing to do. Also, some non-religious people think we should be careful about making euthanasia too easy because this could be a 'slippery slope' to ending people's lives for the wrong reasons.

Should people have the right to die?

## Active Learning

1. Draw up a table which sets out the arguments for and against voluntary and involuntary euthanasia.

2. Many opponents of euthanasia are religious people, though they would accept allowing someone to die. Choose two religions you have studied and find out what their views on euthanasia are. Display your findings. (Remember that many religious people support euthanasia and many scientists oppose euthanasia.)

3. Carry out a survey asking people about their views on voluntary and involuntary euthanasia and report what you find in a small project.

4. Many people make a 'living will', which explains what they would like to happen to them if they were in a PVS or clinically brain-dead. What would you want done? Explain the reason for your wishes.

 **Progress Check**

1. Answer the following:
   a. What is euthanasia?
   b. What is the difference between voluntary and involuntary euthanasia?
   c. What does it mean to say that life is sacred?
   d. What is a PVS?
   e. Is there a difference between killing and letting a person die? What is it?
   f. Why might a religious person support or oppose euthanasia?

2. Debate this statement in class: 'If you have no quality of life, then it should be up to you when and how your life comes to an end.'

3. Design a poster which either supports or opposes euthanasia. You can use voluntary or involuntary euthanasia as the basis for your poster.

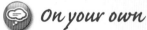 **On your own**

1. Have a look at the websites of some organisations which explain pro- and anti-euthanasia opinions, such as:
   - www.bbc.co.uk/ethics/euthanasia/
   - www.euthanasia.com/
   - www.euthanasia.cc/europe.html

   What arguments do they use to support these views? (You could also look into the campaign by MSP Margo MacDonald, who wants to change Scots law so that a person can choose to die.)

2. The 'quality of life' argument says that there can come a point in life where its quality is so bad that it's no longer worth living. What for you is a good quality of life?

# 7

# Spring celebrations

*It's Alva in the foothills of the Campsies. Kelly and Anya are third years looking forward to another day off school – the May Day holiday…*

**Kelly:** Hey Anya, we're going shopping on Monday – want to come? Oh… wait a minute… it's May Day. You'll be celebrating the harvesting of the sacred turnip or something…?

**Anya:** No need to be nippy! But, yeah, I will be celebrating Beltane – the coming of the summer months.

**Kelly:** So what's that one then, toasting tourists inside a wicker doll?

**Anya:** Not funny. No, we hoist a maypole and deck it with ribbons. Then we dance around it to welcome the spring and the return of life to Earth.

**Kelly:** Maypole eh – is that not a bit…?

**Anya:** Again, you rush headlong into the wrong conclusions because of your warped little mind. The maypole is simply a way to remind ourselves that without the things the land provides for us, we couldn't live at all. I know you think everything grows on supermarket shelves, but even in the modern world we still rely on the forces of nature to provide us with food – and if it doesn't grow, we don't.

**Kelly:** Hey, remember in primary when Erin was May Queen? Now that was funny!

**Anya:** Nasty again. We will have a May Queen – and it's quite an honour to represent the newness of spring. You get gifts too, they're quite nice actually.

**Kelly:** Hey, why don't you go to the big Beltane fire festival in Edinburgh? I read that it's the biggest of its kind in the country.

**Anya:** It is, but we don't really think that it's a proper Beltane celebration. It mixes up all sorts of ideas from everywhere – and we prefer to do things our own way.

**Kelly:** It's a great party though.

**Anya:** It probably is, but if you ask me, you go to one too many parties these days. Isn't it time to start thinking about what really matters in life?

**Kelly:** I do. And on that point, maybe you could come to the shops after your celebrations…?

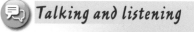
### Talking and listening

- Do you celebrate the coming of spring in any way?
- Do you think people who live in towns and cities have 'lost touch' with the cycles of nature?
- Why do you think schools in Scotland still have a May Day holiday?
- How much do you know about where your food comes from?
- Why is the Beltane celebration linked to growth in nature?

## Beltane traditions

In times past, Beltane was linked to a god called Bel and was celebrated with fire – which was called tane. Fire was seen as something which purified things in readiness for the important growing seasons of the spring and summer months. So the celebration was linked to fertility, which is all about reproduction and growth.

It wasn't only the fertility of the land which was celebrated, but of people too. This was the time for relationships between two people to blossom – so that life could go on as it always has. Celebrations involved symbols and ideas linked to the concept of fertility, and the idea of the death of the old and the birth of the new. It was a way to mark another stage in the year as well as another stage in life's journey.

Modern Beltane festivals still observe many of the old rituals and some add new things too, the origin of which isn't always clear. After the long dark winter, people were happy at the freedom which the coming of the spring represented and so celebrated it joyfully, and this is reflected in modern celebrations. There are May Queens, hand-fasting, green men, hawthorn wreaths, bonfires and torches. Even where people don't really know much about the Beltane festival, a May holiday is still observed – another example of how ancient beliefs are still there under the surface of modern practices.

### Active Learning

1. Visit the website of the Peebles Beltane festival (**www.peeblesbeltanefestival.co.uk/**) and the Edinburgh Beltane celebrations (**www.beltane.org/**). Use some of the images to create your own display about Beltane celebrations. What do these events have in common and what are the differences between them? What symbols are present during these celebrations and what do they stand for?

2. Carry out some research about May Day celebrations around the world. You will often find that these are linked to political ideas – why is this? You could use a world map to plot what happens where.

3. Ask as many people as you can why we have a holiday around the first of May. How many people know why?

4. The celebration is all about the return of life in the springtime. If you can, take a walk around your local area and make a note of everything which suggests that winter is over and springtime is on its way.

## On your own

1. This celebration is closely linked to the land and the crops which grow there. Find out which crops are sown in Scotland at this time of year and when they will be harvested. Also find out which crops are 'in season' at this time of year.

2. Have a look around your local supermarket or food shops and find out how many of your foods are produced locally as opposed to coming from far away. Is the year-round availability of food making us forget our link to the land?

## Progress Check

1. Answer these questions:
   a. What is a maypole and how is it used in Beltane celebrations?
   b. What is Beltane celebrating?
   c. What did the word Beltane originally stand for?
   d. Why is fire linked to Beltane?
   e. What kind of plant is usually used to make Beltane wreaths?
   f. What other things happen at May Day celebrations around the world?

2. In the past, Beltane celebrations were sometimes banned. Discuss as a class why you think this was. Does your school or community celebrate Beltane in the same way that it celebrates Halloween?

3. Design a poster for a Beltane festival in your area.

Hi, I'm Lexi – let me tell you about how we celebrate Easter in Greece. The parties and parades begin weeks before Easter. Some last all through the night and great fun is had by all. But as Easter day itself approaches, things take a more serious turn, and the mood gets a lot more serious and gloomy – it's almost kind of spooky.

On the Thursday before Easter Sunday, it's quite dark and gloomy everywhere. And on the Friday you can hear the sound of long, slow mournful bells ringing everywhere – it can be quite depressing. It's like someone has died, or is about to… which

I suppose makes sense after all. This continues over onto Saturday where the normally cheery churches are also dark and dismal. On Saturday night pretty much everyone is in the churches. The streets can be like ghost-towns. Everyone stands in the dark church holding an unlit candle. There's just one flame on the altar – a very special flame.

At midnight the priest – who's also been very downcast up to now, brightens up and shouts out loudly 'Christos anesti!', which means 'Christ is risen!' We all reply 'Alithos anesti!', which means 'He is risen indeed!'. At this point the bells peal out joyfully and the flame is passed from candle to candle. Before you know it, the church is as bright as can be and the candles light up everyone's faces. There might be fireworks and people's car horns sounding as you leave the church.

The next day, it's party time again with a great meal (usually a whole roasted lamb) and there's a great party atmosphere. We go to church again first though, and crack red eggs on the steps of the church before returning home to party. The mood is now completely different to the last few days – and we look forward to the coming summer months too. It's definitely my favourite time of year…

So a 'Kalo Pascha' to you!

### 🗨 *Talking and listening*

- Do you celebrate Easter? Why? How?
- Are there any similarities between this celebration and Beltane?
- Do eggs play any part in your Easter celebrations? Why?
- In what way might an egg be a good symbol for springtime?
- What do Christians believe happened at the first Easter?

1. Imagine you've been to Greece at Easter. Write a short postcard home describing the Easter celebrations.

2. Eggs are an important symbol of Easter in Greece and also in other places where the arrival of springtime is celebrated. Why is this? Make a display of different ways in which eggs are used as symbols of springtime around the world. You could also look up the word 'Oestre' and see how this links to Easter.

3. You are likely to have studied the Christian Easter story already in school. Produce a table matching the events of the first Easter to the modern symbolism of Easter celebrations (for example, egg rolling = stone in front of Jesus' tomb being rolled away).

4. Create your own class display of objects associated with Easter (in Greek Orthodox tradition as well as other Christian traditions, and Beltane too). You could add to this as you continue to study this section of the course.

## Easter celebrations

In Greek Orthodox Christianity, Easter is really the most important celebration of the year. It celebrates the resurrection of Jesus from the dead and so the start of Christianity. However, it also involves practices and traditions which may be even older than Christianity. This is another example of how people celebrate the end of the winter months and the start of the new world which spring brings.

Many of the celebrations are about the new life of Jesus after the death of his old one. But many traditions also celebrate new life generally, and the hope that spring has arrived to bring life back to what seemed to be a dead land. You can't get more of a symbol of new life than an egg after all. Spring is the time of year when life seems to return to the land. New crops are planted and the trees return to blossom. It must have seemed to people in the past that whatever caused life had returned from its 'death' during the winter.

As well as the Christian symbolism, there are other symbols too. The red eggs represent the blood of Jesus and cracking them represents Jesus breaking free from his tomb. The person whose egg cracks last is also thought to be the one who will be most lucky for the rest of the year!

1. Answer these questions:
   a. How are churches in Greece different before and after Easter?
   b. Describe what happens during the Saturday service in the church.
   c. What do Greeks say to each other as Easter Sunday arrives?
   d. What is done with the eggs on Easter Sunday?
   e. What is likely to be eaten at the Easter Sunday meal and why?
   f. What are Greek Christians celebrating at Easter?

2. Discuss in your class how the Greek Easter celebrations are a mixture of celebrating Christianity and springtime all at once.

3. Create a series of quiz cards about Easter celebrations in Greece. This should cover:
   ■ what is done and why
   ■ the Christian meanings of the events
   ■ how this celebrates springtime.
   You could then have a class quiz.

## On your own

1. Watch a video of Greek Easter celebrations and write down anything you find out which you didn't know already. You should be able to find a suitable video on YouTube.

2. There are many special foods eaten in Greece at Easter. Find out what they are and what they symbolise (try www.ultimate-guide-to-greek-food.com/greek-easter.html). Perhaps you could make some of these in Home Economics.

I am Benjamin and I am four and three-quarters. We're having a Pesach party. Mummy has cleaned the house and I helped. Mummy doesn't usually like cleaning. We looked for bready stuff. There were even crumbs under the sofa cushions. Mummy sold them. Who would want to buy that? Mummy also sold some of our knives to our neighbours. She says she'll buy them back next week… that's odd. Then we have the big dinner.

When I'm at the table Daddy always tells me to sit up, but at this dinner he tells me to sit back and look all floppy like I'm lying in bed. There are four big cups of wine which people drink – that's not as much as usual, but I prob'ly shouldn't tell you that. Mummy gets us all to look for some more bready stuff and, even though she's cleaned up so well, it always seems to be me who finds it and I get a prize.

Then there's a special plate. I think it's called the Sadie plate, and there's stuff on it. There's an egg, but there aren't any toast soldiers. It's boiled and when we eat it there's a real stink. There's a bit of roast meat, but we don't eat that – 'specially not my sister cos' she's a vegetable-tarian and she gets a beetroot instead. There's herby things too and they're bitter, but not as bad as broccoli. There's a thing like apples and nuts all mashed up. It's like baby food and I don't want it cos' I'm not a baby. There's a vegetable and some lettuce too which makes my sister happy. We do lots of hand washes in the middle of all this and there's prayers and wee songs and stuff.

Then I get to be the star of the show cos' I have to ask Grandpa a big question: 'Why is this night different from all other nights?' Grandpa's very old, I think he's about two hundred years old, and he forgets things. He tells me the same story every year – I think he's forgotten that he told me last year, but I pretend that he's not told me already. The story is a bit scary – about a Pharaoh who had slaves and who wouldn't let them go. Then he did, then he didn't, then he did. But only after some horrible things happened to him like boils and stuff. People even got killed which isn't very nice. Grandpa tells me that it's all to remind us that we are free. It's alright for him, but I don't always get to do what I want…

### 🗨 Talking and listening

- How often does your family gather together around a table for a meal?
- Do you have any special celebrations at springtime?
- When are you likely to have a special meal as a family?
- Do you think of yourself as 'free'?
- How important do you think it is to remember the past?

# The Pesach Seder

Pesach, or Passover, reminds Jewish people of the story of the escape of the Israelites from slavery in Egypt (called the exodus). They believe that G-d freed them from slavery after sending ten plagues to make the Egyptian Pharaoh change his mind about letting them go. The last plague was the death of first-born children. The Israelites avoided this by marking their homes so that the angel of death (sent by G-d) would pass over their homes, leaving their children unharmed.

These events are remembered through a great many symbolic actions during the Passover meal, also called Seder. In this event, Jewish people remind themselves of the story and pass this on to their children. The meal is a way for Jewish people to thank G-d for the various ways in which he has delivered them from trouble throughout Jewish history. At this event they give thanks to G-d for keeping them free.

## Active Learning

1. Even for Jewish people, planning and organising a Passover meal can be a complicated event. Have a look at www.chabad.org/holidays/passover/default_cdo/jewish/Passover.htm and use the information to produce your own instruction book for celebrating Passover.

2. Retell the exodus story about the Israelites escaping from Egypt in your own way. It could be a cartoon, animation, short video or anything else you choose. You will be able to find the story at the website above.

3. In what ways are people in the world today free and not free? Are there still people living in slavery? Produce your own display about this. You could also include ways in which someone your age is 'free' and 'not free'. The website www.amnesty.org.uk/ will help you here.

4. Jewish people believe that it is important to keep history alive by passing it on to children. How does your family (or community or school) keep its history alive and what is the value of this? Discuss in class and compare your findings.

1. Answer these questions:
   a. What roles does Benjamin play in the Passover celebration?
   b. What is on the Seder plate?
   c. What does each item on the Seder plate represent?
   d. Why is Passover celebrated?
   e. What happened at the first Passover?
   f. Why do Jewish people want to remember the past?

2. Discuss this statement: 'We should forget the past and live only for the present.'

3. Write your own A–Z of the Passover which covers as many of the events as possible (for example, 'A is for Apples, all mashed up in the paste…')

 **On your own**

1. Jewish history is full of times when freedom seemed to be the last thing available. Find out more about one period in Jewish history where freedom was an issue. You could look at:
   - the Maccabean revolt
   - the Babylonian exile
   - the Holocaust
   - the Diaspora.

2. At the end of every Seder, the family says 'Next year in Jerusalem'. What is this statement about and why is the issue of Jerusalem a complicated one in the world today?

Here in Thailand we celebrate Wesak as the day of the Buddha's birthday. Some people also remember his death and his enlightenment on this day, so it can all get a bit complicated. It's also pretty hard to know when the day is because it's all to do with the Moon and stuff. I just wait until the date's announced! We get to the temple before the Sun's even up and we meditate there. All over the streets there are lanterns lit – probably standing for the Buddha's enlightenment. One really fun thing is the release of loads of caged birds. These fly free in their hundreds and symbolise becoming free from attachment. There are even candlelit processions in the evening with all the monks chanting.

In China, we also celebrate the Buddha's birthday, enlightenment and death. We choose the date based on the full Moon and there are dragon processions and everything. We also bathe Buddha statues in water or just pour it over the statue. This is to symbolise our washing away the things which attach us to life. In Japan, they do the same, but they use tea there! We take gifts to the temple and light joss sticks there. We also give money away to the poor so that everyone is happy.

In Sri Lanka we also celebrate Wesak. We don't just release birds from cages though, we release all kind of animals! This reminds us that we are all aiming for release from the endless cycles of birth, death and rebirth. There are stalls on the streets giving away free food and everybody is very happy. Some people think that Buddhism is not a very cheery religion because we're always meditating and sitting quietly, not dancing about, but at Wesak the idea is to be happy and enjoy yourself and help others to do so too.

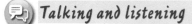

### Talking and listening

- When is your favourite celebration of the year?
- What kinds of things do you celebrate during the year?
- What do you think about celebrating someone's death in a happy way?
- Do you think of Buddhism as a religion where people are quite serious?
- What features does this celebration share with other springtime celebrations?

## Wesak celebrations

Oddly enough, the celebration of Wesak was only agreed in 1950 at a worldwide meeting of Buddhists. There had been celebrations before this though. In the different countries where Buddhism was present, the celebrations took slightly different forms.

For Buddhists, the Buddha is the person who shows us how to escape the endless sufferings of life and achieve true happiness. Buddhists aim to escape this cycle of life and achieve Nirvana (or enlightenment) and so be truly happy. But Wesak shows that Buddhists value happiness in this life too!

Wesak, like many religious celebrations around the world, is celebrated in different ways in different countries. This shows that as religions spread around the world, they take on something of the character of the places they end up. Buddhism in the cold high mountains of the Himalayas is a little different to Buddhism in the warm steamy forests of Thailand, for example. This shows something important: religions have cultural features as well as religious ones, and it is sometimes hard to separate out what is part of a religious faith and what is part of a culture's customs and traditions.

## Active Learning

1. Make your own display of different Wesak celebrations around the world. Show how in countries where Buddhism exists, they celebrate in similar and different ways.

2. In Wesak, many features that are common to other celebrations at this time of year in other religions are present. Compare the celebrations you have looked at in this section by producing a table setting out the different aspects of the celebration. You could use the headings below to organise your table:
   - parties and special foods
   - light (such as candles and fire)
   - the importance of new life or freedom in life
   - remembering special people or special events.

3. Find a video clip of some Wesak celebrations – you should easily be able to find one on YouTube. Write your own script for the video and show the film in class while reading your commentary.

4. The cycles of the Moon are used to decide when Wesak occurs. In what other religions can you find lunar cycles being used and what are they used to decide? Why do you think the Moon is used in this way?

1. Answer the following questions:
   a. When is Wesak celebrated and why?
   b. Why are animals sometimes released at Wesak?
   c. What might happen to Buddha statues and why?
   d. What things are given away for free at Wesak and why does this happen?
   e. How is the date of Wesak decided?
   f. What do Wesak celebrations tell us about how religion changes as it spreads around the world?

2. Discuss this question: 'If all life is suffering, should Buddhists be celebrating in a happy way?'

3. You have one minute (exactly) to tell someone everything you know about Wesak. Who in your class can get the most information about Wesak into that minute?

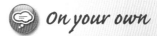 *On your own*

1. You should already know about the life and teachings of the Buddha. What do you know about the circumstances of his death though? Find out about the events and what Buddhists believe they tell us about the religion of Buddhism.

2. Design a Happy Wesak card using images and ideas linked to the celebration.

*We're in Inverness, where Rachel is talking to her friend Ravinder about what she's doing during the Easter holidays…*

**Rachel:** So, you going anywhere? We're off on a cruise around Lanzarote.

**Ravinder:** Again? Your dad own a ship or something?

**Rachel:** Nah… What about you?

**Ravinder:** Well it'll be New Year in a couple of days.

**Rachel:** Eh? In April?

**Ravinder:** Aye, that's when we celebrate the first new harvest from the fields.

**Rachel:** Not up here we don't. There's still snow for goodness sake – that's why we're off to the Sun!

**Ravinder:** Yeah, I know, it's kinda chilly up here. But in the Punjab where Sikhism comes from, it's already warm and sunny and the first crops are ready to harvest.

**Rachel:** Sounds like a good reason to celebrate… You know I like my food.

**Ravinder:** Aye, mostly deep-fried in batter with a pickled onion on the side!

**Rachel:** Hey, that's my culture you're on about.

**Ravinder:** Anyway, it's not just about food, it's about the founding of the Khalsa too.

**Rachel:** Oh. We did that in RME, didn't we? That's when that guy chopped off people's heads…

**Ravinder:** 'That guy' was Guru Gobind Singh, one of our most important leaders. And he didn't chop off anyone's head – he just pretended to.

**Rachel:** Classy… That's what passes for comedy in the Punjab, is it?

**Ravinder:** This from a girl who needs a joke explained to her ten times before she gets it… No, he was just testing whether anyone was brave and faithful enough to offer to sacrifice themselves for their faith. And he found five who did, and they became the first members of the Sikh Khalsa.

**Rachel:** Oh aye, now I remember… And they had to wear stuff, didn't they?

**Ravinder:** Wear stuff…? They had to wear five objects to show that they were Sikh warriors and that they would defend the faith. And they got Singh, which means lion, and we girls got Kaur, which means princess.

**Rachel:** Yeah, my dad calls me princess sometimes… so lame.

**Ravinder:** I think he's being ironic, Rachel.

**Rachel:** Really?

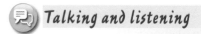

### Talking and listening

- Is April a more sensible time to celebrate a New Year than January?
- Are there any celebrations of food harvests where you live? When do these take place?
- Do you wear any clothes which show that you are part of something?
- Have you ever had to 'prove yourself' at something?
- What things are you prepared to stand up for in your life?

ਭੂੰ ਕਾਰ ਅਜ ਹਾਂ ਹੀਲਤੇ ਦਰ ਗੁਜ਼ਸ਼ਤ ॥
ਹੁਲਾਲ ਅਸਤ ਬੁਰਦਨ ਬ ਸ਼ਮਸ਼ੀਰ ਦਸਤ ॥

*All modes of redressing a wrong having failed, Raising of sword is pious and just.*

## Vaisakhi celebrations

In the Punjab region of India, there were celebrations in April to mark the first harvests of the year. This was an important event as it provided the food which people needed to survive, and so great festivals were held at this time. The Sikh faith was founded by Guru Nanak, the first Guru, in the sixteenth century, and he was followed by nine more Gurus (ten counting the Guru Granth Sahib, of course). The last human Guru, Gobind Singh, founded the Sikh Khalsa in the seventeenth century at a Vaisakhi celebration, where he did indeed invite people to offer their heads for the faith.

So, in present-day Sikhism, Vaisakhi is a celebration of the New Year, the new harvest and the founding of the Khalsa all in one. It is a very happy occasion, very colourful, and involves lots of feasting and enjoyment – including very energetic dancing known as bhangra and gidda. Streets are decorated and there are processions to the Gurdwara where there are special services. Many Sikhs choose to become members of the Khalsa at this time and may even be baptised into the faith using the sweet nectar or Amrit. From now on, they pledge to defend their faith with their lives.

### Active Learning

1. Retell the story of the founding of the Khalsa. You can do this through drama, a multimedia presentation or a simple set of illustrations.

2. The Punjab region of India is the centre of the world of Sikhism. Find out more about this area and its geography and history. How did the Sikh faith develop? What political issues are present in the Punjab today?

3. Find a clip of bhangra dancing on the Internet and describe what you see. Perhaps you could try it out.

4. The Vaisakhi festival is also important in Hinduism and Buddhism. Find out why this is and how it is celebrated in these faiths.

1. The golden temple at Amritsar is the centre of Sikhism, but has also been the site of tension in the region. Find out about the role this temple plays in Sikhism and how it has been linked to political, religious and social tensions in the area. Look at:
   - www.sgpc.net/golden-temple/index.asp
   - http://sacredsites.com/asia/india/amritsar.html

2. Find a recipe for amrit and make some.

1. Answer these questions:
   a. When is Vaisakhi celebrated and what might seem unusual about this for Scottish people?
   b. Describe the events of the founding of the Khalsa.
   c. What was the aim of Guru Gobind Singh's actions?
   d. How do modern-day members of the Khalsa identify themselves?
   e. What happens at a typical Vaisakhi celebration?
   f. Why is this festival important to Hindus and Buddhists too?

2. Discuss the similarities and differences between Vaisakhi and the other springtime celebrations you have studied in this section.

3. Create a rhyming poem about the events of the founding of the Khalsa which begins: 'Guru Gobind Singh did a very scary thing…'

# Christianity:
# A world religion

I am a member of the Iona Community, which is a kind of religious order. A bit like monks and nuns, that kind of thing, but we don't wear any special clothes and we live and work in the normal everyday world. For all you know, I might be sitting next to you in class today – though we don't keep our identity secret or anything like that so you'd probably know. We're not some secret association guarding a holy grail or anything.

Basically we try to live our lives according to a set of rules about our faith, which help us to structure our lives in a meaningful way. We do five things, in fact:

- First of all we pray and read the Bible every day. Not all day of course, and we do read other things; we think it's very important to pray for others and the world and to learn more about our faith. But we're not just holy Henrys sitting around praying all day.

- We also promise to use our money wisely and share it where we can. We give ten per cent of the money we have left over after we've paid all our bills and the like to helping others in different ways.

- We also promise to use our time wisely: for example, getting a balance between work and leisure in our lives.

- Then there's our commitment to social justice and equality. We think that justice, peace and looking after God's creation are all very important. We commit ourselves to making the world a better place in whatever ways we can – anything from writing letters to MSPs, to protesting against injustice on the streets.

- Finally, we promise to meet together as individuals and families to help support each other in our lives. Each year, in May, we have to write down our intention to stick with the Rule of the Community.

Being part of the Iona Community gives my life a focus and a structure. It reminds me that even in the middle of a busy and sometimes troubled world, I am part of a community which shares my ideals and beliefs and is working for a better world. And let's face it, the world could be a lot better.

(Based on information from www.iona.org.uk/ iona_rule.php)

## Talking and listening

- Do you follow any rules in your life (which you have decided upon)?
- How much of your money do you give away to those in need?
- Is the balance of your life between work and leisure right?
- Do you protest against injustice and inequality?
- What do you do to make the world a better place?

## Origin of the Iona Community

Although the Community is based in Glasgow, it originated on the Island of Iona just off the Isle of Mull. On this tiny island, Saint Columba (or Colum Cille as he was known) arrived from Ireland bringing Christianity to the Pictish peoples who lived in what's now Scotland. This took place way back in the sixth century.

It is said, however, that Colum Cille didn't set off with the intention of becoming a religious missionary… He had to leave Ireland in rather a hurry because of some serious trouble he got himself into. And, in fact, his missionary work was a way for him to try to make up for the trouble he had caused! However, he founded an abbey and one still stands there today.

Members of the Community can be found all over Scotland (and in other countries), where they live their lives according to the Rule of the Community and try to put their Christian faith into action. As well as working in normal jobs in the wider world, the Iona Community also offers retreats and events in Iona. You can go there for a week to reflect on your life and its meaning, and learn more about how the Christian faith might help you and the world in which you live.

## Active Learning

1. Find out more about Saint Columba and how he brought Christianity to Scotland, as well as how it spread. You could prepare a display about your findings or a mini project.

2. Create a holiday brochure-type article about the retreats and events you can attend on Iona. You can find information on the Community's website at www.iona.org.uk/

3. The Community believes that its members should fight for justice, peace, equality and freedom for people experiencing poverty and unfairness. Create a collage of images and stories from newspapers showing the kinds of things that members of the Community might think should be tackled in the world.

4. The Iona Community also tries to find ways to make Christian worship more contemporary and more meaningful – especially for young people. How do most Christians in Scotland currently worship and what different ways of worshipping has the Iona Community explored? (See the Community's Wild Goose section at www.iona.org.uk/ wgrg_home.php)

**On your own**

1. Members of the Iona Community think of Iona as a very peaceful and spiritual place. Create a slideshow of images of Iona and choose suitable music as backing for the display.

2. What other Christian religious orders are there in the world today and in what ways are they similar to or different from the Iona Community?

**Progress Check**

1. Answer these questions:
   a. In your own words, describe the five rules followed by members of the Iona Community.
   b. Who was Colum Cille and what did he do?
   c. What kinds of events happen on Iona?
   d. In what ways is the Iona Community trying to make Christianity fit into the twenty-first century?
   e. What specific issues do members of the Community try to speak out against?
   f. What must members of the Community write each year?

2. Discuss these opposing statements:
   ■ Living a life according to a religious rule is a good way to help make sense of the world.
   ■ Living a life according to a religious rule is out of date and out of touch with reality.

3. Create an information sheet about the five rules which members of the Iona Community follow.

Looking around today you would hardly believe that the things that happened to my parents and those of their generation really occurred… but they did. There were times when things were calm, and Christians were left to get on with their beliefs as long as they were quiet about it. But there were other times when there were terrible crackdowns on all things religious. Priests and worshippers would be rounded up and taken away. Many ended up in the terrible gulags of Siberia, from which most never returned. Some lost their lives right here in the cities. They say that they were tortured and murdered by their fellow countrymen for refusing to give up their beliefs.

As a child at the time, it was all just a game for me – hiding away in the woods with my parents and their friends, worshipping in the open air. I had no idea that our lives were at risk by doing this. At times beautiful churches, which had stood for centuries, were robbed of their holiest items. Others were just closed and used as factories. Some were simply turned to rubble. People could be rounded up and imprisoned for nothing more than owning religious books. There were even people who tried to smuggle books – such as the Bible itself – into our country, and risked their lives doing so.

You see, the Soviet state made atheism the official 'belief' of the country, and tried to persuade everyone that Christians (in fact, people of any religion) were enemies of the state. They were to be rooted out and destroyed before they could do any harm with their ridiculous beliefs. And yet… when the Soviet empire began to crumble, one of the first things that happened was that the churches grew again, and grew in strength. You see, faith had been there all the time, just waiting for the right conditions so that it could blossom, and blossom it did. That sorry period in our history is over – thank God, literally.

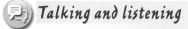 **Talking and listening**

- Should people be allowed to believe what they want and express their beliefs as they like?
- Should what people believe be decided by governments? Can they do this?
- Would you risk something for your beliefs?
- Do you think that trying to stop people believing things is ever effective?
- Is religious belief a natural part of what it means to be human?

# Christianity in Russia

Christianity has a long history in Russia. Eastern Orthodoxy is one of the oldest branches of the faith and was, for much of Russia's history, closely tied to Russia's rulers and the people of Russia.

However, after the Russian revolution, Christians became a persecuted group in the USSR (Union of Soviet Socialist Republics), which replaced old Russia. Under the communist Government of the USSR, atheism was the state 'religion' and Christianity went through many periods of persecution, some much worse than others.

The Government taught that religion was just a fantasy – a dangerous one – which stopped people being all that they could be. So, in one way or another, they tried to stamp it out. Many Christians tried to keep their faith in secret, while others were more open about it and risked very serious punishments indeed. It wasn't just in the USSR either – Christians were under attack in all the countries of the Eastern bloc which the USSR controlled.

Eventually, in the 1980s, the USSR collapsed all over what was known as the Soviet bloc. Christianity once again became a central feature of these new countries and their people. It seems like no matter how hard you try to stop people believing what they want, it's really impossible to do so.

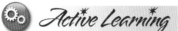

## Active Learning

1. On a map or Eastern Europe, mark which countries were part of the USSR and the Eastern bloc. You could also add the dates when each country returned to independence. Also, if you can find it, include information about the number of people following religions, including Christianity, at the different stages of the rise and fall of the USSR.

2. Prepare your own mini project about the Russian Orthodox Christian Church today. Explore the beliefs, values, practices and traditions of the Church and include illustrations and facts and figures.

3. Throughout the time of the USSR and still in Russia today, many other Christian denominations exist apart from the Orthodox Church. Prepare a pie chart showing the number of Christians in Russia today and which denominations they are from.

4. During the Soviet era, many people did indeed try to smuggle Bibles and religious books into the Eastern bloc – taking great risks in doing so. Find out about one person who did this (Brother Andrew) and prepare a factsheet on his activities. See www.inspirationalchristians.org/brother-andrew/

**Progress Check**

1. Answer these questions:
   a. How were many Christians (and people of other religions) treated in the USSR?
   b. How did people try to continue with their religious life?
   c. Why did the USSR behave this way towards religious people?
   d. What happened to Christianity when the USSR collapsed?
   e. In which other countries ruled by the USSR were Christians often treated badly too?
   f. Does Christianity in Russia today prove that you can't stop people being religious?

2. Discuss this statement: 'The success of Christianity in modern Russia proves that religion is a natural part of being human.'

3. Write a short magazine article called 'Christianity in Russia: then and now.'

 **On your own**

1. Find out about the beliefs of communism and decide for yourself whether you think the Government of the USSR were following communist beliefs when they tried to stamp out religion.

2. Other religions were also persecuted during the Soviet era. Find out more about one other religion which also suffered as Christianity did.

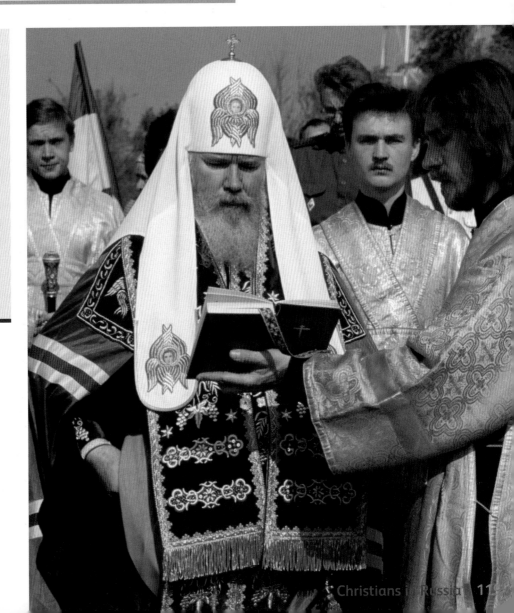

# 38 Christianity in Ethiopia

You might have thought that the job of guarding one of the world's greatest secrets and – if you believe it – one of the most powerful objects in the world would have been given to a military force of well-armed troops. But only one frail old man lives in the tiny church where this object is said to be. He is in Axum, in Ethiopia. He was chosen for this task as the guardian by the previous guardian as he lay dying. When this old man finally reaches his last moments of life,

he too will announce the name of the new guardian.

Inside this tiny building is said to be an object so powerful that it was carried before great armies in the past, and helped them to utterly annihilate their enemies. It is said that God himself set out the instructions for this object, and inside it is contained the very tablets of stone upon which the Ten Commandments were originally inscribed. If such an object is truly there, then it would

be the archaeological find of all time. And if it has any of the power that it is said to have… well… what would that mean?

Each year, Ethiopian Christians parade through the streets with imitations of this object, celebrating its great power. But the real thing – if it is there – never leaves the small church, and it is said that it never will. Only this one man, the guardian, is permitted to see it… and he will take its secret to his grave.

## 🗨 Talking and listening

- Could such an object exist in this small church?
- Why do you think only one old man is in charge of this church?
- What do you know about the Ark of the Covenant?
- If this object is there, should it not be shared with the world?
- Why do most people like a bit of mystery?

# The Christian Church in Ethiopia

Most Christians in Ethiopia do claim that the Ark of the Covenant is kept there. The Bible story of the Ark is that it was made as a container for the Ten Commandments following the instructions given by God to Moses, and is a powerful object in its own right. Ethiopian churches have replicas of the Ark in them, and each year the replicas are paraded through the streets at a festival called Timkat, which also celebrates the baptism of Jesus in the river Jordan.

Ethiopian Christianity has a long history and is one of the Orthodox Christian traditions. How it got there is not completely clear. Some think that the first Christians were converts from Judaism, which had been a strong force in the country since the return of the Queen of Sheba from King Solomon's Israel. Others argue that the faith was brought by two Syrians who had been shipwrecked there and, after a period as slaves, became powerful people who converted the Emperor to Christianity. Others say that the evangelist Philip converted a traveller from Ethiopia who returned home and spread his new faith.

When Islam was expanding to cover the rest of north Africa, Ethiopia remained Christian, and Christianity remains strong in this country. Ethiopian Christians also have a presence around the world, and there are even Ethiopian churches in prime locations right next to the holiest sites of Christianity in Jerusalem itself.

 *Active Learning*

1. Find out about the Ark of the Covenant. The instructions for its creation are in the Bible (Exodus 25:10–16). Describe what was kept in it (the Ten Commandments, Aaron's Rod and a Jar of Manna). Explain how it helped the Israelites at Jericho and in what other ways it is believed to show the power of God. Create your own illustrated information sheet about this. There's a History Channel clip about the Ark at **www.youtube.com/watch?v=YOqLpT6HKzY** Perhaps you could make your own replica of the Ark.

2. The Timkat festival in Ethiopia centres on baptism and the carrying of the Ark replicas (Tabot). You can find videos of the events at **www.youtube.com/watch?v=OXJPbGb_8Qk** Watch the video clips and describe what you see.

3. Create a presentation on Ethiopian Christianity which explains the ways in which it is similar to and different from other versions of Christianity you have studied.

4. The Ethiopian Orthodox Church is one of the groups which look after the Church of the Holy Sepulchre in Jerusalem. Find out why this church is said to be an important Christian site and which other Christian groups share this responsibility with the Ethiopian Church. Display your findings.

1. Answer these questions:
   a. What do some believe is kept at the small church in Axum?
   b. What beliefs are there about this object and what it contains?
   c. How does the Ethiopian Church celebrate this object each year?
   d. What different theories are there about how Christianity came to Ethiopia?
   e. Which site in Jerusalem does the Ethiopian Church help protect?
   f. What beliefs are held about this site?

2. Discuss this statement: 'If the church in Axum does contain the Ark, then they should reveal this to the world so that the object can be scientifically tested.'

3. Imagine you could speak to the guardian of the church in Axum. Write a list of questions you would ask him about the contents of the church. What answers do you think he might give?

 **On your own**

1. The Ark has appeared in many movies – most famously *Raiders of the Lost Ark*. Watch one of these movies and write about how the Ark is portrayed.

2. The Timkat festival also celebrates the baptism of Jesus. Find this Bible story and explain why Christians think it is a particularly important event in the life of Jesus.

I'm heading off to join the Army's work in the Solomon Islands. This is a group of nearly a thousand islands just east of Papua New Guinea. This will be the 123$^{rd}$ country in which you will find Salvationists spreading the faith and helping those in need.

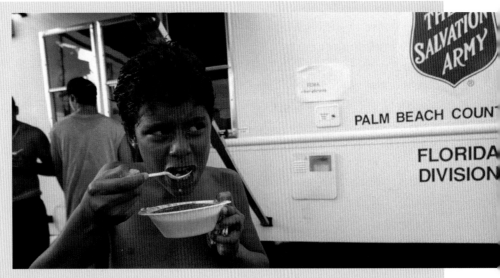

I work here in Canada. I work in our addictions services. Here we help drug addicts to come off drugs and turn their lives around for the better. In our big cities, homelessness and drug addiction often go hand in hand. We try to help people get back on their own two feet and live a productive, drug-free life.

*In Pakistan we have been making sure that people have special tents to see them through the cold winter. After the floods of 2010, many people were without homes and these tents might just help them survive the winter months.*

Here in Queensland Australia, people have had some drastic weather recently – floods then cyclones. We've been here, helping people out wherever we can, even if it has been nothing more than serving them up a good breakfast.

*My job with the Army is a tough one. I work to make people aware of the exploitation of children around the world, such as child prostitution, and* encourage people to speak out against it and act against it whenever they can. In one country where we work, it is estimated that 575,000 children are involved in child prostitution.

Here in Iraq we are helping to rebuild schools for girls. The country hasn't yet recovered from its years of war and the education of girls is still an issue in places.

*In Indonesia, we operate hospitals to provide healthcare for those in need.*

All through sub-Saharan Africa, we work closely with other agencies to help people get access to the food they need to survive. It may be the twenty-first century, but around 25,000 people still die each day through hunger or problems linked to hunger.

*My role in the Army is to help others evangelise throughout* the world. Our practical work in helping people is vital, but so too is our task of giving everyone in the world a chance to hear the word of God.

(Based on materials found on the Salvation Army International website at www.salvationarmy.org)

## Talking and listening

- Have you ever encountered members of the Salvation Army?
- How would you recognise a member of the Salvation Army?
- Should Christians take a 'military' approach to their faith?
- Should Christians get involved in difficult social issues or just worship?
- Is it right to spread your beliefs around the world?

## Active Learning

1. On a world map, mark the places where Salvationists currently operate. Choose four or five countries where they work and write a note about what they do there. An interactive world map of the work of the Salvation Army is available at www.salvationarmy.org/ihq/www_sa.nsf/vw-sublinks/331AED2D11F74E4780256E4B002EB72D?openDocument

2. Choose one area of the Salvation Army's social work and design an illustrated information sheet about this work.

3. Choose one area of the Salvation Army's evangelising programme and write a series of questions and answers (FAQs) about this.

4. Choose one story of the work of the Salvation Army (you will find many examples on their website) and report on it in the form of a magazine article for people your age. For example, the story of the two villages on Papua New Guinea who had been fighting each other for 20 years and were helped to make peace by trading in their weapons for Bibles!

## The Salvation Army internationally

The Salvation Army began in the streets of east London, among the poor and those in need. Its founder, William Booth, thought that putting the world right was like fighting a war against evil and so he ran his branch of Christianity along military lines. Salvationists are officers, soldiers, generals and captains. They wear uniforms and are as well organised as any army anywhere – even their magazine here in the UK is called *War Cry*.

They currently operate in 123 countries around the globe – in almost every area of the world – and their work ranges from helping the homeless to helping those with drug and alcohol addictions to fighting against sex-trafficking and the exploitation of children.

As well as their hard-hitting social action, they also believe that their role is to make sure that everyone in the world has the chance to hear the Christian Gospel in a way that he or she can understand. They believe that everyone should have the opportunity to become a Christian if they want to, which they believe will transform them and save them. Salvationists think that such spiritual transformation is more likely to be achieved where you work with the 'totality' of a person's life. Someone is more likely to be open to the Gospel if their ordinary needs in life are met first.

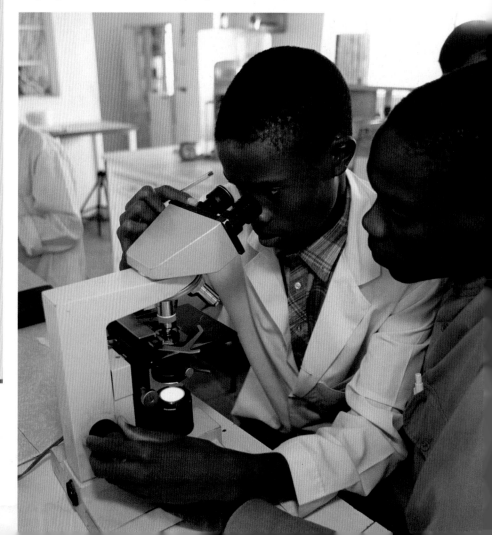

'You drive the women of my people from their pleasant homes. You take away my blessing from their children for ever.'

*Micah 2:9 NIV*

CALL TO PRAYER

*for*
Victims of Sex Trade Trafficking

SUNDAY
26 SEPTEMBER 2010

Sex trade trafficking is still a gross offence upon the earth. Please use this weekend to raise awareness, raise your voices and raise funds against this outrage.

Designed by Berni Georges. Published with permission of the Salvation Army International Headquarters, London, UK

## On your own

1. Choose one of the areas of work the Salvation Army is involved in here in Scotland and carry out your own research into it. You should be prepared to report on your findings.

2. Draw up a set of questions you would like to ask a Salvationist. Perhaps you could invite someone in to your school to answer them or post them on the Salvation Army website.

## Progress Check

1. Answer these questions:
   a. Name ten countries where the Salvation Army works.
   b. Describe two things the Salvation Army tries to help people with.
   c. What is evangelising?
   d. How is the Salvation Army organised?
   e. Why does the Salvation Army want to give people the opportunity to become Christians?
   f. What is the Salvation Army's magazine called and why does it have this name?

2. Discuss this statement: 'It would be good if more Christians were like the Salvation Army.'

3. Use the letters of the phrase 'the Salvation Army' to make an acrostic which describes their work in the world.

Look around you… Look at what you own. You will find that much of it was made in China. We are growing in strength and power as a nation, and some say that very soon we will be even more powerful in the world than the USA. Our economy is strong and our people are committed to making a better life for themselves through education and good, old-fashioned hard work.

Some say that Hong Kong (which has now been returned to us) is the wealthiest city in the world. And yet, even though much of our country is glittering with the flashing lights of material success, we are still a deeply spiritual people. My family were, for most of their long history, followers of our own Chinese religions. But I became a Christian many years ago and my family has followed me in this – even though my mother also worships other gods too. But that's not unusual in China.

I am a member of the Three-Self Patriotic Movement, which is a Protestant Christian group. We are recognised by the Government as a Christian group. There have been times when the Government was less keen on recognising Christianity, and there are still some tensions in this area between the Government and some Christian groups, but I think you're better to try to work with the authorities than to go against them.

They say that things move slowly in Chinese history, so I am prepared to take my time in waiting to have my faith respected by those in power. This approach is working, I think. In some countries I understand that the number of Christians is going down… but not here in China. The Church is definitely growing among every age group and new churches are being built all the time. Perhaps the future of Christianity lies here…

💬 *Talking and listening*

- How much of what you own was 'made in China'?
- What do you know about the religions other than Christianity which exist in China?
- Do you think that the number of Christians in Scotland is going down?
- Why might Christianity be on the increase in countries such as China?
- Why might there still be some opposition to Christianity in countries such as China?

# Chinese Christianity

Christianity has been present in China for many years. In fact, some say that it reached China within 100 years of the death of Jesus. It has had its followers there ever since, though for many periods of Chinese history it was under attack because it was thought to be a non-Chinese influence on people.

Many missionaries went there from the West and there has always been a rather uneasy relationship between what was seen by Chinese rulers as a 'Western' religion and the 'Chinese way'. During much of

China's history, Christianity, like other religions, was discouraged by the authorities. For them, religion stood in the way of progress and of making China a great nation. Again, some Christian groups had a more difficult time than others and many Christians simply left the country.

However, the faith remained and is growing today. There are registered Christian groups and unregistered ones – each with different levels of control exercised by the Government. And there are different views about what this means in practice. There are all kinds of Christian groups in the country: Catholics, Protestants, Orthodox and all sorts of denominations within these three groups. It remains to be seen how Christianity might develop as China grows in power and influence in the world.

## Active Learning

1. Chinese Christianity has often had trouble in translating Christian ideas into the Chinese language. For example, the word 'God' has sometimes been translated as 'the emperor above'. Search the Internet and find out how key Christian words are translated into something which can be understood in China. (The website www. chinese-word.com/chinese/z_bible.html might help.)

2. Produce your own timeline of Christianity in China, matching it up with the history of China more generally. Try to show periods where Christianity thrived and where it had more difficulty being accepted.

3. Many Chinese Christian communities have started up in countries where Chinese people have settled. Find one example of this (if there's one in your home town that would be best to use) and prepare a presentation on this church's worship and way of life. For example, see:
   ■ www.cece.org.uk/English/archive.htm (Edinburgh)
   ■ www.refinersfire.co.uk (Glasgow)
   ■ www.aberdeenchinesecc.org.uk/ (Aberdeen)

4. Find out more about the Three-Self Patriotic Movement and create a report about your findings. What are their key beliefs and values, and what Christian practices do they engage in?

**Progress Check**

1. Answer these questions:
   a. Name one Christian group in China.
   b. When do some think Christianity reached China?
   c. Why has Christianity sometimes had difficulty in China?
   d. What kinds of Christian denominations are present in China?
   e. Describe one example of how a Christian key term has been translated into Chinese.
   f. Where might you find Chinese Christians in Scotland?

2. Discuss this statement: 'It is the right of a Government to keep the activities of religious people in its country under control.'

3. Write out a list of seven things you have learned about Chinese Christianity.

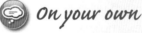 *On your own*

1. China is a vast country with a huge population and many different groups of people living within its borders. Christianity is only one of many religions present there. Find out which religions exist in China and how many followers each one has.

2. Chinese language characters are quite complex because they convey ideas. Choose one or two of the Christian terms which have been translated into Chinese (from your work in *Active Learning* activity 1) and write it out in Chinese characters. You should include an explanation in English too.